THE SPIRIT OF
REVELATION

THE SPIRIT OF REVELATION

Joseph Fielding McConkie

Deseret Book

Salt Lake City, Utah

First printing March 1984
Second printing April 1985

Library of Congress Cataloging in Publication Data

McConkie, Joseph F.
    The spirit of revelation.

    1. Revelation (Mormon theology) I. Title.
BX8643.R4M29   1984   231.7′4   84-1705
ISBN 0-87747-990-9

Contents

Preface   vii

Acknowledgments   viii

1   Revelation and Salvation   1

2   Revelation: Types and Purposes   10

3   Prepare Yourselves   21

4   Seeking Revelation   33

5   A Personal Urim and Thummim   49

6   Understanding Personal Revelation   60

7   A Bible! A Bible!   71

8   The Second Witness   95

9   Revelations of the Restoration   105

10   The Pearl of Great Price   114

11   Manifestations of the Spirit   121

Index   131

Preface

When Moroni appeared to the youthful Joseph Smith during the night and early morning of September 21 and 22, 1823, the Smith family was living in a small two-room cabin. An extension had been made on one of the sides (undoubtedly a room for his parents) and a loft constructed where Joseph and his brothers slept. With a family of eleven sharing these quarters, Joseph would not have been alone when Moroni made his three appearances that night. The family slept through it all. We are left to wonder how often we in like manner have "slept" through marvelous manifestations, not knowing the spirit of revelation.

Three times while Samuel slept the Lord called, and three times Samuel went to Eli, saying, "Here am I; for thou calledst me." "Now Samuel did not yet know the Lord," we are told, "neither was the word of the Lord yet revealed unto him." Recognizing what was taking place, Eli instructed Samuel to return to his bed, and when the voice spoke again, Samuel was to say, "Speak, Lord; for thy servant heareth." (1 Samuel 3:1-10.) It was time for Samuel, the child of faith and obedience, to awaken to the things of the Spirit.

Such was the challenge given by Paul to the Roman saints. "Now it is high time," he said, "to awake out of sleep: for now is our salvation nearer than when we believed." The night was spent and the day was at hand, and Paul desired all who were of the household of faith to arise and clothe themselves in the "armour of light." (Romans 13:11-12.)

Since the time of Christ, no one has done more to illuminate the world with the light of revelation than the Prophet Joseph Smith. If revelation is the subject, then Joseph Smith is the world's great schoolmaster. He spoke as one having authority. He testified of Christ, whom he had seen and with whom he had conversed. Joseph Smith studied at the school of the ancient prophets. Their curriculum was his curriculum. As they had learned gospel principles in dreams and visions, so he learned of them in dreams and visions; as they had listened to the whisperings of the Spirit, so he listened to the whisperings of the Spirit; and as they had been instructed by angels, so he was instructed by angels.

Learning of the spirit of revelation from his father, Nephi was encouraged to seek the same blessings. Through the teachings and experiences of the Prophet Joseph Smith we learn of that same spirit and are similarly encouraged to seek the same understanding and blessings. With Joseph Smith (who has penned more revelation than any prophet of whom we know) as our guide, let us seek to know and understand the spirit of revelation.

Acknowledgments

Special appreciation is extended to my student secretary, Barbara Tanner. The painstaking work was hers. I am also indebted to my father, Elder Bruce R. McConkie, for his careful reading of the manuscript, his enthusiasm, and his encouragement.

Chapter One

Revelation and Salvation

Salvation cannot come without revelation. (Joseph Smith, HC 3:389.)

No principle associated with the message of the restoration is of greater importance than the simple yet sublime announcement that "God speaks!" It is not to academic halls and their learned professors that we turn to give credit for an announcement of such marvel. Nor is it to chapels, cathedrals, or synagogues, and to those professing to be the stewards of the divine word, that we are able to render thanks, for in unison the litany of all such is that the heavens are sealed and that God speaks to us only through the past. But such was not the testimony of an unlearned frontier boy who, in the purity of youth, sought to know God. It was not the testimony of one unsoiled by the traditions of men, one who could read the sacred writ and believe its promises, one to whom James, the Lord's brother, had addressed himself nearly two millennia earlier as he wrote his inspired epistle to scattered Israel promising that any who sought wisdom of God would receive it if only they would ask in faith.

All Are Invited to Ask of God

The message of James was as thunder to the soul of Joseph Smith. "Never did any passage of scripture come with more power to the heart of man than this did at this

time to mine," declared this youthful reader. "It seemed
to enter with great force into every feeling of my heart. I
reflected on it again and again." (Joseph Smith–History
1:12.) And thus the words were imprinted upon his heart
and mind: "If any of you lack wisdom, let him ask of God,
that giveth to all men liberally, and upbraideth not; and it
shall be given him." (James 1:5.)

Surrounded on every side by the "war of words" and
the "tumult of opinions," young Joseph came to the reali-
zation that the answers he sought were not to be found in
the wisdom of men, for, he said, "the teachers of religion
of the different sects understood the same passages of
scripture so differently as to destroy all confidence in
settling the question by an appeal to the Bible." (JS–H
1:12.) Yet the Bible pointed to the source of truth. Did it
not testify that for more than four thousand years God
had freely spoken to his children? Did it not declare God
to be the same yesterday, today, and forever? Did it not
promise that those who asked would receive? And had
not James assured that the heavens would respond without rebuke or reproach?

"At length," said Joseph Smith, "I came to the conclusion that I must either remain in darkness and confusion,
or else I must do as James directs, that is, ask of God."
(JS–H 1:13.) The story is well known to every Latter-day
Saint. Joseph asked, the heavens were opened, God
spoke, and he promised to continue to do so. Those who
seek the wisdom of God, in faith, can still expect an answer.

Joseph Smith shared his experience with a minister,
who told him "that there were no such things as visions or
revelations in these days; that all such things had ceased
with the apostles, and that there would never be any
more of them." (JS–H 1:21.) It would appear that the
good reverend, like countless others of whom he was but
the spokesman, had forgotten the promise of Joel that in
the last days "young men shall see visions." This was to be

a day, Joel said, when the Lord would pour out his spirit upon all flesh. To dramatize the fact that the spirit of revelation was to be universally enjoyed, Joel said that young men and young women would prophesy, while old men would dream dreams, and that even servants and handmaids would be the recipients of heavenly treasures. (Joel 2:28-29.)

The Bible Promises Continuous Revelation

Have men become so bold and vain as to revoke the very promises of heaven? Is it for mortal man to seal the covers of the Bible or the lips of God? And "what power," might we ask, "shall stay the heavens?" To this Joseph Smith answered, "As well might man stretch forth his puny arm to stop the Missouri in its decreed course, or to turn it up stream, as to hinder the Almighty from pouring down knowledge from heaven upon the heads of the Latter-day Saints." (D&C 121:33.) And to those who would make of God a mute, Joseph asked, "Does it remain for a people who never had faith enough to call down one scrap of revelation from heaven, and for all they have now are indebted to the faith of another people who lived hundreds and thousands of years before them, does it remain for them to say how much God has spoken and how much he has not spoken? We have what we have, and the Bible contains what it does contain: but to say that God never said anything more to man than is there recorded, would be saying at once that we have at last received a revelation; for it must require one to advance thus far, because it is nowhere said in that volume by the mouth of God, that He would not, after giving, what is there contained, speak again; and if any man has found out for a fact that the Bible contains all that God ever revealed to man he has ascertained it by an immediate revelation, other than has been previously written by the prophets and apostles." (*History of the Church* [HC] 2:18.)

The promise that the spirit of revelation was to continue is found throughout the Bible. John the Revelator declared that "the testimony of Jesus is the spirit of prophecy." (Revelation 19:10.) He foretold the mission of two prophets who were to "prophesy a thousand two hundred and threescore days" in the streets of Jerusalem, where, like their Master and many of the prophets of old, they would seal their testimony with their blood. (Revelation 11:3.) John also foretold the coming of an angel "having the everlasting gospel to preach unto them that dwell on the earth, and to every nation, and kindred, and tongue, and people." (Revelation 14:6.) Thus it is our testimony that the gospel of Jesus Christ revealed anew in our day will go forth and fill the earth "as the waters cover the sea" (Isaiah 11:9), for such is the testimony of "all his holy prophets since the world began" (Acts 3:21).

God Can Be Known Only by Revelation

The ancients made no profession in knowing God without revelation, nor can we. Indeed, God stands revealed or he remains unknown. The Bible system for gaining the knowledge of salvation was threefold: personal revelation, the testimony of living witnesses, and the acceptance of all available scriptural writ. The order of their listing is of no moment; what *is* significant is that all three elements were always present. Could you imagine a Bible prophet professing his faith while rejecting the inspired writings of earlier prophets? For instance, Jeremiah declaring his faith in God while rejecting the writings of Isaiah? Could you imagine Peter, James, and John rejecting the testimony of Abraham, Isaac, and Jacob? Or Isaiah professing a faith in previous scriptural writings but denying the possibility that God would speak to anyone else now that he had spoken to him? Is it possible to picture Paul declaring a belief in the Old Testament writers but refusing to acknowledge the Twelve whom Christ had chosen? Can you picture Peter and the apostles professing Christ on the strength of the Old Testament prophecies alone—making no profession to any personal witness of the Spirit?

We need not multiply illustrations—the point is obvious: the believing peoples of the Bible professed personal revelation; they sustained their leaders as prophets, seers, and revelators; they reverenced the writings of the righteous who preceded them as scripture; and they freely added to it.

Such was the pattern followed by the Savior himself. He entertained angels and studied the sacred scrolls. He was true to the testimony of the prophets who came before him. He reverenced their teachings and taught their doctrine. He came, he said, not to destroy the law or the prophets, but to fulfill both. Rather than sealing the heavens to future generations, he commissioned others to carry on his work, promising them the spirit of revelation. (John 14:26.) Nor was this promise given exclusively to the Twelve. The doctrine of Christ was that "everyone that asketh, receiveth; and he that seeketh, findeth; and unto him that knocketh, it shall be opened." After he had so taught, his disciples reported that when they sought to teach and testify of him, they were rejected by a people professing righteousness and claiming no need for what any man could teach them. "We have the law for our salvation," the disciples were told by their fellow Jews, "and that is sufficient for us." Christ in turn instructed these missionaries to respond by asking, "What man among you, having a son, and he shall be standing out, and shall say, Father, open thy house that I may come in and sup with thee, will not say, Come in, my son; for mine is thine, and thine is mine?" (JST, Matthew 7:13-17.)

In a day when the message of continuous revelation is again being rejected by people professing righteousness and salvation by virtue of inspired instructions given in ages past, this exchange between Jesus and his disciples seems remarkably relevant. Well might the missionaries of this day ask of such people, "Would they refuse counsel to their own children because they had already given instruction to their older brothers and sisters?" What child of a loving parent would return to his home seeking sustenance and instruction only to be refused because such help had been given previously? Thus the Savior asked, "What man is there of you, whom if his son ask bread, will he give him a stone? Or if he ask a fish, will he give him a serpent? If ye then, being evil, know how to give good gifts unto your children, how much more shall your Father which is in heaven give good things to them that ask him?" (Matthew 7:9-11.)

By closing the canon of scripture and then taking refuge in it, people past and present have justified their refusal to listen to the voice of the Redeemer and his chosen servants. Yet the scriptures testify that there have been times when people listened, and they prophesy that ours is a day when God will speak again and that the elect will hear his voice. (D&C 29:7.) Such is the day spoken of by Jeremiah when he said that a people would rise up saying, "Surely our fathers have inherited lies, vanity, and things wherein there is no profit. Shall a man make gods unto himself, and they are no gods? Therefore, behold, I will this once cause them to know, I will cause them to know mine hand and my might; and they shall know that my name is The Lord." (Jeremiah 16:19-21.) Describing the same day through the pen of Isaiah, the Lord said, "My people shall know my name: therefore they shall know in that day that I am he that doth speak: behold, it is I." (Isaiah 52:6.)

Joseph Smith's Mission Foretold

As Elijah placed his mantle upon Elisha and thus designated him as his rightful successor, so the prophetic language of Isaiah, which was first a mantle in which the

Savior and his ministry were clothed, was to be placed in turn on a latter-day prophet, one who was to do the works of the Savior as Elisha was to do the works of Elijah. Thus, much of Isaiah finds a second fulfillment, or rather its complete fulfillment, in the events of the last days. A prophet, known to Isaiah and described by others of the ancient prophets even by name (2 Nephi 3:15), was to "bring Jacob again to the Lord" and to "restore the preserved of Israel." The very language of this prophet—his "voice of warning," which was to be unto the ends of the earth—was foreshadowed by Isaiah: "Listen, O isles, unto me; and hearken, ye people, from far; The Lord hath called me from the womb; from the bowels of my mother hath he made mention of my name." (Isaiah 49:1.)

Doctrine and Covenants 1:1, which is the Lord's preface to the compilation of revelations testifying of Joseph Smith and his divine call to restore Israel, contains this phrase: "Hearken ye people from afar; and ye that are upon the islands of the sea, listen together." This section of the Doctrine and Covenants, like many that follow, is a symbol of the very events that it announces: it introduces the prophet of the restoration and the latter-day gathering of Israel by weaving together threads from the writings of Israel's ancient prophets as they foretold this very story. Thus the weaving together of these scattered prophecies into the tapestry of the restoration typifies the manner in which Israel itself will be gathered together in one.

No Salvation without Revelation

Section one continues by announcing that the "voice of the Lord is unto the ends of the earth, that all that will hear may hear." All such are directed to prepare for that which is to come "for the Lord is nigh; [and again the language will be that of Isaiah:] and the anger of the Lord is kindled, and his sword is bathed in heaven, and it shall fall upon the inhabitants of the earth. And the arm of the

Lord shall be revealed; [now, as we shall see, the language becomes that of Moses:] and the day cometh that they who will not hear the voice of the Lord, neither the voice of his servants, neither give heed to the words of the prophets and apostles, shall be cut off from among the people." (D&C 1:11-14.)

Moses had prophesied to Israel of a prophet who would arise from their midst speaking the words of the Lord. Those who failed to listen to the words of that prophet were warned that the Lord would "require it" of them. (Deuteronomy 18:15, 18.) Peter testified that that prophecy was filled in Christ, and that those who did not accept the testimony of the apostles as they taught of him would be "destroyed from among the people." (Acts 3:23.) To the nation of the Nephites, the resurrected Christ said, "Behold, I am he of whom Moses spake, saying: A prophet shall the Lord your God raise up unto you of your brethren, like unto me; him shall ye hear in all things whatsoever he shall say unto you. And it shall come to pass that every soul who will not hear that prophet shall be cut off from among the people." (3 Nephi 20:23.) Christ also spoke of a future day when the record of the Nephites as a witness of him would come forth through the hand of a chosen servant, and that whosoever would not believe the testimony of that record, "(it shall be done even as Moses said) they shall be cut off from among my people who are of the covenant." (3 Nephi 21:11.)

The Scriptures Promise Personal Revelation

Thus we see the Bible and the Book of Mormon teaching the same truth. There is no salvation in the revelations of the past. They offer encouragement and help, they inspire and instruct, they point out the path we are to follow—but they do not excuse us from the journey. Each generation must have its own witnesses that Jesus is the Christ, and each individual must have his own experiences with the spirit of revelation. Peter testified that Jesus was the Christ, and the Savior responded, "Blessed art thou, Simon Bar-jona: for flesh and blood hath not revealed it unto thee, but my Father which is in heaven." (Matthew 16:17.) Yet that revelation granted by the Holy Spirit to Peter will not save me any more than Peter's baptism will wash away my sins. If I desire a remission of sins, it is for me to repent and be baptized, not rely on the repentance and baptism of another; and if I desire to know God, it is for me to obtain that revelation from the Holy Ghost, as Peter did. His good works will not save me nor will Judas's evilness damn me. It is for me to seek and obtain the blessings of heaven as have the children of the Lord in all ages past. Theirs was a God who would speak to all who sought him in righteousness, and so is mine.

Chapter Two

Revelation: Types and Purposes

I thank God that I have got this old book [the Bible]; but I thank him more for the gift of the Holy Ghost. I have got the oldest book in the world; but I have [also] got the oldest book in my heart, even the gift of the Holy Ghost. (Joseph Smith; HC 6:308.)

For the purpose of our consideration, we will divide revelation into four categories: institutional, stewardship, shared, and personal. By *institutional revelation,* we mean the canon of scripture known to Latter-day Saints as the standard works. By *stewardship revelation,* we mean those inspired promptings, in their multitude of forms, that are granted to sustain and direct us in our various offices and callings as we labor in the Lord's vineyard. The phrase *shared revelation* is used to describe experiences had in company with others. By *personal revelation* is meant those spiritual directions intended for us individually or for our families. Let us briefly consider the nature and purpose of each.

Institutional Revelation

The plan of salvation is universal. It remains the same for all men in all ages. Like its Author, it changes not; it is the same yesterday, today, and forever. Whether revealed to Adam or to Joseph Smith, it is the same. Eternal principles are not in flux; they can neither be added to nor taken from. Such principles once revealed stand for all and are for all time; they need not be granted anew to each individual or to each succeeding generation. In the written form they are known to us as scripture; collected together, they are known to us as the canon of scripture or as the standard works.

These inspired writings are intended to be used in teaching the gospel in all the world. From these books all men will be judged. Acceptance of them and compliance with the doctrines declared by them is essential to salvation. They are the mind, the will, and the word of the Lord to all men. They are the standard by which all doctrines and philosophies are to be judged. In them is found the fulness of the saving principles of the gospel of Jesus Christ. At the present time they consist of the Bible (Old and New Testament), the Book of Mormon, the Doctrine and Covenants, and the Pearl of Great Price. We have the promise that as we prepare ourselves and become worthy of it, these books will be expanded to include other revelations from biblical times, the sealed portion of the Book of Mormon, and, of course, the will of the Lord as it is manifest to our living oracles.

Though the nature of these revelations is such that they need not be continually reannounced from the heavens, it is the right—yea, the responsibility—of every soul to seek a personal confirmation of their verity by that same Spirit from whom they came. To those born in the household of faith—that is, families where these principles are lived—this knowledge comes as a natural inheritance. This accords with the Savior's promise that those who "do his will" shall "know of the doctrine." (John 7:17.) For these, no dramatic spiritual display is necessary; they have been raised on the fruits of the Spirit. Theirs is a quiet assurance, one best described with such words as calm, serene, and peaceful. On others, the Spirit may have a far more visible effect.

Explaining this principle, Joseph Smith said that the Holy Ghost was "more powerful in expanding the mind, enlightening the understanding, and storing the intellect with present knowledge, of a man who is of the literal seed of Abraham, than one that is a Gentile, though it may not have half as much visible effect upon the body; for as the Holy Ghost falls upon one of the literal seed of Abraham, it is calm and serene; and his whole soul and body are only exercised by the pure spirit of intelligence; while the effect of the Holy Ghost upon a Gentile, is to purge out the old blood, and make him actually of the seed of Abraham. That man that has none of the blood of Abraham (naturally) must have a new creation by the Holy Ghost. In such a case, there may be more of a powerful effect upon the body, and visible to the eye, than upon an Israelite, while the Israelite at first might be far before the Gentile in pure intelligence." (HC 3:380.)

Though experiences will differ, all are entitled to a spiritual confirmation of the verity of the scriptural canon. Christ himself declared that "whosoever shall believe in my name, doubting nothing, unto him will I confirm all my words, even unto the ends of the earth." (Mormon 9:25.) Moroni assured that all who would read and ponder the scriptures "with a sincere heart, with real intent, having faith in Christ," will have the truth thereof manifest to them "by the power of the Holy Ghost. And by the power of the Holy Ghost ye may know the truth of all things." (Moroni 10:4-5.) After having given a great discourse from the scriptures, Alma gave the formula whereby one obtains this spiritual confirmation:

"Do ye not suppose that I know of these things myself? Behold, I testify unto you that I do know that these things whereof I have spoken are true. And how do ye suppose that I know of their surety? Behold, I say unto you they are made known unto me by the Holy Spirit of God. Behold, I have fasted and prayed many days that I might know these things of myself. And now I do know of myself that they are true; for the Lord God hath made them manifest unto me by his Holy Spirit; and this is the spirit of revelation which is in me." (Alma 5:45-46.)

Stewardship Revelation

No one is asked to labor on the Lord's errand without the Lord's direction. Certainly without such direction none could credibly profess to represent him. "We believe," states the fifth Article of Faith, "that a man must be called of God, by prophecy, and by the laying on of hands by those who are in authority, to preach the Gospel and administer in the ordinances thereof." All, great and small, are to be called by prophecy and to accomplish their labors under the direction of the same Spirit. It is for the Lord to choose his own agents, and it is for him to direct their labors.

The pattern is clearly established in the manner in which Jesus chose the Twelve in the Old World. Each was sought out individually, and of each he was later able to say, "Ye have not chosen me, but I have chosen you, and ordained you." (John 15:16.) Further, he carefully instructed them in what they were to say and do, for as his agents, they were to do the bidding of none else. Again the scriptures contain the pattern. The Nephite twelve, finding the multitude at Bountiful too great to preach to, divided it into twelve groups. Each apostle then instructed a group, which we are told was done in the "same words which Jesus had spoken—nothing varying from the words which Jesus had spoken." (3 Nephi 19:8.) And to those who go forth to teach the gospel in our day the Lord has said, "Let them journey from thence preaching the word by the way, saying none other things than that which the prophets and apostles have written, and that which is taught them by the Comforter through the prayer of faith." (D&C 52:9.) All are to conform to this standard, for the Lord has declared that "the Spirit shall be given unto you by the prayer of faith; and if ye receive not the Spirit ye shall not teach." (D&C 42:14.) Nothing independent of the spirit of revelation is acceptable; indeed, the Lord has declared, "If it be by some other way it is not of God." (D&C 50:18.)

No legitimate claim can be made to represent God, which at the same time rejects the principle of revelation. Without revelation, there could be no priesthood. Priesthood, which by definition is the power and authority to act in the name of God, could hardly be held by someone whom God had not commissioned and to whom he would not speak.

The Lord's house is a house of order. No man calls himself to the apostleship, and in like manner no man receives revelation for the apostles. This principle is consistent at all levels of Church government. Revelation is freely granted within the bounds of one's stewardship, while none can rightfully profess revelation for those who preside over them. Every man is to learn his own duty and stand in his own office; none are to assume prerogatives that go beyond the bounds of their callings. The classic illustration of this principle is the story of the man who came to Brigham Young claiming to have a message for him, which he said he had received from an angel. Brigham Young directed the fellow to return home with the instruction that if the angel came again, he was to tell him to go back to hell whence he came.

Shared Revelation

There is a spiritual power found in the united purpose of the Saints that is not otherwise experienced. To his disciples anciently, the Savior declared: "If two of you shall agree on earth as touching any thing that they shall ask, it shall be done for them of my Father which is in heaven. For where two or three are gathered together in my name, there am I in the midst of them." (Matthew 18: 19-20.) Renewing that promise in our day, the Lord said: "As it is written—Whatsoever ye shall ask in faith, being united in prayer according to my command, ye shall receive." (D&C 29:6.) This promise is the rightful inheritance of all who have hands laid upon their heads by legal administrators to grant to them the gift of the Holy Ghost.

From the beginning of time, revelation has been a shared experience. Of our first parents we read, "Adam and Eve, his wife, called upon the name of the Lord, and they heard the voice of the Lord from the way toward the Garden of Eden, speaking unto them, and they saw him not; for they were shut out from his presence." (Moses 5:4.) Three years prior to Adam's death, a great conference of the Church was held in the valley of Adam-ondi-Ahman. All the righteous posterity of Adam were assembled to witness the appearance of the Lord Jesus Christ, who administered comfort unto father Adam. (D&C 107:53-55.) Throughout all scriptural history the pattern thus established of the heavens opening themselves to faithful couples and to the great congregations of the Saints has been followed.

One is immediately reminded of the appearance of the resurrected Christ to the two on the Emmaus road and to the apostles and their families in the upper room; of his appearance to more than five hundred brethren in Galilee; of the great multitudes who witnessed his appearance at the Temple Bountiful; and of the promise of his appearance to those of the Lost Tribes. As to our dispensation, the principle varies not. One immediately thinks of the season of Pentecost that attended the dedication of the Kirtland Temple; of the transfiguration of Brigham Young, witnessed by thousands; and even more recently of June 1, 1978, when the First Presidency and the Twelve all heard the same voice and received the same message, as the Lord directed that the privilege of the priesthood be extended to worthy males of all races.

God, who rejoices in manifesting himself to the congregations of the righteous, is wroth with those who will not seek such experiences. Moses "sought diligently to sanctify his people that they might behold the face of God; but they hardened their hearts and could not endure his presence; therefore, the Lord in his wrath, for his anger was kindled against them, swore that they should not enter into his rest while in the wilderness, which rest is the fulness of his glory. Therefore, he took Moses out of their midst, and the Holy Priesthood also." (D&C 84:23-25.)

We cannot suppose that the anger of the Lord is less in our day with those posing as his ministers who declare the heavens to be sealed, or with those among the Latter-day Saints unwilling to seek and live for such experiences.

It must be evident even to those who are spiritually timid that association with the faithful and participation with the Saints as they assemble in worship will inevitably bring with it the treasures of the spirit, for as the Lord has said, "Where two or three are gathered together in my name, as touching one thing, behold, there will I be in the midst of them—even so am I in the midst of you." (D&C 6:32.)

Personal Revelation

There are no secret sources where gospel knowledge is concerned; as saving principles are for all, so the library of the Spirit is open to all. This was the doctrine of the Prophet Joseph Smith, who in turn had learned it from the apostle James. All who lack wisdom are invited to ask of God; scores of scriptural passages so testify, with no qualifications as to office, position, or social standing. When Martin Van Buren, then the president of the United States, asked Joseph Smith how Mormonism differed from all other religions, he was told that "we differed in [the] mode of baptism, and the gift of the Holy Ghost by the laying on of hands. . . . All other considerations were contained in the gift of the Holy Ghost." (HC 4:42.)

The privilege of those possessing the gift of the Holy Ghost to have full access to the library of the Spirit is effectively illustrated by Elder Bruce R. McConkie in remarks to students at Brigham Young University, assembled in the George Albert Smith Fieldhouse. "All the revelations of eternity are here," he said, "but you and I who have assembled in the devotional are probably not receiving them. This fieldhouse is full of the visions of eternity, and yet we are not viewing visions at this moment, but we could.

"Now analogously, this great fieldhouse is full of great symphonies. There are symphonies played here, and our ears are not hearing them. There are sermons that are being preached, but we do not hear them. Yet if we had the means and the ability, we could tune in and hear the symphonies and see the visions.

"One day in Hobart, in Tasmania, I said to my missionaries, 'We will hold our meeting on the top of Mount Wellington'—a tremendous mountain that overlooks the city and the bay. They did not realize I was serious at first, but after I told them that all great men, Moses, the brother of Jared, Nephi, and so on, climbed mountains, they consented. So while it was scarcely dawn we assembled at the foot of the mountain and spent a good many weary hours climbing to the top.

"On the top we found some television relay stations. Since we were there, we gained permission to be shown through. There was a very bright young man who, using language that we did not understand, but speaking with a tone of authority, explained in detail the things that were involved in relaying television broadcasts. I was totally unable to comprehend or understand what was involved, but I knew that the thing did take place.

"That night, down in the valley again—two of my

young sons were with me—we stayed in a room where there was a television set. They tuned the wave band of that set to the broadcast that came from the top of the mountain. We saw in the room projected before us, in effect, the visions of eternity.

"The same thing applies in radio. If we had a radio here today and tuned it to the proper wave band, we would hear the symphonies that are being broadcast into this building. Or if we looked on television we would see in effect the visions that are coming forth in a similar way.

"Now in the same sense, if at any time we manage to tune our souls to the eternal wave band upon which the Holy Ghost is broadcasting, since he is a Revelator, we could receive the revelations of the Spirit. If we could attune our souls to the band on which he is sending forth the visions of eternity, we could see what the Prophet saw in Section 76, or anything else that it was expedient for us to see. It would all happen by compliance with law, by conformity to the eternal principles that God has ordained.

"Now I am not able to explain how this takes place. I know that the laws exist; and like the young man who explained the television broadcast without really knowing how the pictures go through space, I also can state, as one having authority, that these things do take place in the spiritual realm, and that it is possible to receive revelation and direction and guidance in our personal affairs." (*BYU Speeches of the Year*, September 29, 1964, pp. 4-5.)

Perhaps no scriptural text better teaches this principle than the introductory verses to Joseph Smith's great vision on the degrees of glory. Here the Lord says that all who fear him, serving him in righteousness and truth to the end, shall enjoy eternal glory. To these he also promises to "reveal all mysteries, yea, all the hidden mysteries of my kingdom from days of old, and for ages to come, will I make known unto them the good pleasure of my will concerning all things pertaining to my kingdom. Yea, even the wonders of eternity shall they know, and things to come will I show them, even the things of many generations. And their wisdom shall be great, and their understanding reach to heaven; and before them the wisdom of the wise shall perish, and the understanding of the prudent shall come to naught. For by my Spirit will I enlighten them, and by my power will I make known unto them the secrets of my will—yea, even those things which eye has not seen, nor ear heard, nor yet entered into the heart of man." (D&C 76:5-10.)

The early history of the Church contains an account of a young elder, who, while en route to his mission, had a marvelous experience in which the heavens were opened to him. Wisely he refrained from sharing the experience with anyone until he was able to counsel with his mission president, at which time he was told that the revelation was for him and was to be kept private. Four years later Joseph Smith, in a great discourse on the nature of God, publicly taught for the first time the doctrine revealed to the young missionary. After the Prophet had publicly declared the doctrine, the elder, Lorenzo Snow, was freed from the restraint placed on him by his mission president, Brigham Young, and it became his right to testify of the truthfulness of the Prophet's doctrine. This he did, capsulizing his experience in the well-known couplet: "As man now is, God once was. As God now is, man may be."

No better illustration could be found to sustain the principle of revelation. All who have the gift of the Holy Ghost and live worthy of it have claim on all the treasures of heaven, nothing withheld. Still, the manifestation of them does not constitute the commission to declare them; rather, it is a sacred stewardship. Only after the Prophet, whose right it is, has declared the doctrine could one in propriety step forth as a second witness.

Applying the Principle

The wealth of the scriptural canon is the legacy of all who will receive it. It has been symbolized as the rod of iron, which, if we hold fast to it, will lead us to the fountain of living waters. (1 Nephi 11:25.) All are invited to drink deeply of those waters. "The Bible, the Book of Mormon, the Doctrine and Covenants and the Pearl of Great Price—each of them individually and all of them collectively—contain the fulness of the everlasting gospel." (Bruce R. McConkie, "Holy Writ: Published Anew," Regional Representative Seminar, April 2, 1982.) Yet until their message is written in our hearts and souls, they are but black ink on white paper. It is for each man, through the aid of the Spirit, to breathe into them the breath of life, and through the application of their truths, to give them flesh and bones. Further, it is the right of all within the bounds of their own stewardship to receive the promptings of the Spirit. One could hardly profess to be on the Lord's errand without the Lord's direction. It is our right, individually and collectively, to experience the manifestations of the Spirit and know the truths of heaven. All the family of God have claim on the attentions of their Father, be they men, women, or children. (Alma 32:23.)

Chapter Three

Prepare Yourselves

Prepare yourselves, and sanctify yourselves; yea, purify your hearts, and cleanse your hands and your feet before me, that I may make you clean; that I may testify unto your Father, and your God, and my God, that you are clean from the blood of this wicked generation. (D&C 88:74-75.)

The powers of heaven cannot be controlled nor handled only upon the principles of righteousness. (D&C 121:36.)

Nothing is as attractive to the Spirit as works of righteousness. Where righteousness is, there the Spirit will be also. Though a gentile, Cornelius was a devout man; he and all his house feared God, prayed daily, and gave generously of their means to those in need. While the heavens remained sealed to tens of thousands of the chosen race, all professing righteousness, an angel of God appeared to Cornelius and declared that his (Cornelius's) alms had "come up for a memorial before God." (Acts 10:4.) As Cornelius learned, it is righteous works that unlock the gates of heaven.

More than the form of godliness is necessary to open the heavens. Through Isaiah, the Lord denounced the united fast of the nation of Israel because it was attended by strife, debate, and the "fist of wickedness." "Is it such a fast that I have chosen?" the Lord asked, "a day for a man to afflict his soul? is it to bow down his head as a bulrush, and to spread sackcloth and ashes under him? wilt thou call this a fast, and an acceptable day to the Lord?" Emphatically responding to his own question, the Lord then said, "Is not this the fast that I have chosen? to loose the bands of wickedness, to undo the heavy burdens, and to let the oppressed go free, and that ye break every yoke? Is it not to deal thy bread to the hungry, and that thou bring the poor that are cast out of thy house? when thou seest the naked, that thou cover him; and that thou hide not thyself from thine own flesh?" To those whose fast embraced good works, this promise was extended: "Then shall thy light break forth as the morning, and thine health shall spring forth speedily: and thy righteousness shall go before thee; the glory of the Lord shall be thy rereward. Then shalt thou call, and the Lord shall answer; thou shalt cry, and he shall say, Here I am." To these the promise was "the Lord shall guide thee continually." (Isaiah 58:1-11.)

Works, not words, give eloquence to prayer. Teaching this principle, Alma said, "If ye turn away the needy, and the naked, and visit not the sick and afflicted, and impart of your substance, if ye have, to those who stand in need—I say unto you, if ye do not any of these things, behold, your prayer is in vain, and availeth you nothing, and ye are as hypocrites who deny the faith." (Alma 34:28.)

The divine injunction is that we have "charity towards all men, and to the household of faith, and let virtue garnish [our] thoughts unceasingly; then shall [our] confidence wax strong in the presence of God." It is those so living who are promised the constant companionship of the Holy Ghost. (D&C 121:45-46.) Spiritual things, the scriptures declare, can be seen and understood *only* by the power of the Holy Ghost, which power God bestows *only* upon those who love him and "purify themselves before him." (D&C 76:116.)

Freedom from Sin Brings Spiritual Power

There are no greater blessings and there is no greater power than what is granted to those called and sent forth by the Lord. To his legal administrators, the Lord has promised that all things are subject unto them, whether they be in heaven or on earth, for the Spirit and the power are theirs. Yet, the scriptures hasten to add, "No man is possessor of all things except he be purified and cleansed from all sin. And if ye are purified and cleansed from all sin, ye shall ask whatsoever you will in the name of Jesus and it shall be done." (D&C 50:27-29.) Because of his unwearyingness in teaching the gospel, Nephi, a son of Helaman, was told by the Lord, "I will make thee mighty in word and in deed, in faith and in works; yea, even that all things shall be done unto thee according to thy word, for thou shalt not ask that which is contrary to my will. Behold, thou art Nephi, and I am God. Behold, I declare it unto thee in the presence of mine angels, that ye shall have power over this people, and shall smite the earth with famine, and with pestilence, and destruction, according to the wickedness of this people. Behold, I give unto you power, that whatsoever ye shall seal on earth shall be sealed in heaven; and whatsoever ye shall loose on earth shall be loosed in heaven; and thus shall ye have power among this people. And thus, if ye shall say unto this temple it shall be rent in twain, it shall be done. And if ye shall say unto this mountain, Be thou cast down and become smooth, it shall be done. And behold, if ye shall say that God shall smite this people, it shall come to pass." (Helaman 10:5-10.)

As the spirit gives life to the body, so the spirit in which every sacrifice is made, every ordinance performed, every covenant entered into, and every prayer offered must give it life. As the body without the spirit is dead, so these sacrifices, ordinances, covenants, and prayers are dead if they are done without that spirit.

"In the final and all-comprehensive sense, the sole
and only way to find and know God is to keep his commandments. As a result of such a course, knowledge and
revelation will come in one way or another until man
knows his Maker. The more obedient a person is, the
clearer his views become, the nearer he approaches his
God, and the more he comes to know those holy Beings
whom to know is eternal life. (John 17:3.)" (Bruce R.
McConkie, *The Promised Messiah*, Deseret Book, 1978,
p. 18.)

Holy Ground

Places have been dedicated and set apart for the very
purpose of allowing man to come into the presence of
God. Such is the purpose of temples. Temples are houses
of revelation. In directing the Saints to build the Nauvoo
Temple, the Lord said, "Let this house be built unto my
name, that I may reveal mine ordinances therein unto
my people; for I deign to reveal unto my church things
which have been kept hid from before the foundation of
the world, things that pertain to the dispensation of the
fulness of times." (D&C 124:40-41.)

Whenever the Lord has occasion to visit a particular
part of his kingdom the place where he will come will be
to the sanctuary that has been built and dedicated for
that purpose, since the temple is the Lord's house. Only
when circumstances have prevented the building of a
temple will the Lord do otherwise. (D&C 124:30.) The
week following the dedication of the Kirtland Temple,
the Savior appeared to Joseph Smith and Oliver Cowdery. To them he said, "I have accepted this house, and
my name shall be here; and I will manifest myself to my
people in mercy in this house. Yea, I will appear unto my
servants, and speak unto them with mine own voice, if
my people will keep my commandments, and do not pol-
lute this holy house." (D&C 110:7-8.) Years earlier he
had said, "Inasmuch as my people build a house unto me

in the name of the Lord, and do not suffer any unclean thing to come into it, that it be not defiled, my glory shall rest upon it; yea, and my presence shall be there, for I will come into it, and all the pure in heart that shall come into it shall see God. But if it be defiled I will not come into it, and my glory shall not be there; for I will not come into unholy temples." (D&C 97:15-17.) "Because all faithful people stand on a footing of total and complete equality, because all receive blessings as a result of righteousness and not of church position or some other eminence, all who are entitled to see the face of the Lord will receive that blessing in the House of the Lord." (Bruce R. McConkie, "The Promises Made to the Fathers," talk given to Provo Temple workers, July 19, 1981, p. 4.)

The concept of a place set apart for the purpose of receiving revelation is not limited to temples. Along with the building of the temple in Kirtland, the Saints were directed to build an office "for the work of the presidency, in obtaining revelations; and for the work of the ministry of the presidency, in all things pertaining to the church and kingdom." Again the instruction followed: "Ye shall not suffer any unclean thing to come in unto it; and my glory shall be there, and my presence shall be there. But if there shall come into it any unclean thing, my glory shall not be there; and my presence shall not come into it." (D&C 94:8-9.)

When Moses approached the burning bush on the mountain of God, the voice of the Lord called unto him, saying, "Draw not nigh hither: put off thy shoes from off thy feet, for the place whereon thou standest is holy ground." (Exodus 3:5.) That act symbolized the removal of the defilement of the world, the laying aside of the pollutions contacted by walking in the way of sin. It announced anew that no unclean thing was to enter into the Divine presence.

There are, then, places of revelation, places that have been dedicated for that purpose, places that have been

kept clean of the pollutions of a sinful world, places
where the Spirit of the Lord can be manifest without restraint. There are also those places where great and noble
souls have walked and where the marvels of the Spirit
have been manifest; there is a Spirit that attends such
places, just as there is a Spirit that attends such people. It
is of such places that the Spirit whispers "the ground
upon which thou standest is holy."

Holy People

After he had brought the nation of Israel out of
Egypt, Moses was commanded to sanctify the people so
that the Lord might appear to them on Mount Sinai. According to Jewish tradition, this sanctification process involved the ordinance of baptism. We know that they had
the authority to baptize even when they had only the
lesser law. (See D&C 84:26-27.) The tradition that they
were baptized at this time accords with the statement of
the Lord to Moses that if Israel "will obey my voice indeed, and keep my covenant, then [they] shall be a peculiar treasure unto me above all people: for all the earth is
mine: And [they] shall be unto me a kingdom of priests,
and an holy nation." (Exodus 19:5-6.) Surely Israel could
not be a covenant people without baptism, and most certainly they could not be a kingdom of priests without
priesthood, and without baptism there is no priesthood.
Of their priesthood role, Edersheim observes: "Just as
the priest is the intermediary between God and man, so
Israel was to be the intermediary of the knowledge and
salvation of God to all nations. And this their priesthood
was to be the foundation of their royalty." (Alfred Edersheim, *Bible History, Old Testament*, Grand Rapids, Michi-
gan: Eerdmans, 2:109.)

Describing Moses' preparations to ascend Sinai and
obtain the revelation of the law, Jewish traditions speak
of his first being clothed in a special garment, which was
an indication of both the favor of God and his protection.

Talmudic tradition associates Moses' ascension with his first being purified; references are made to his being washed, anointed, called with names of honor, and robed in heavenly garments. This was all preparatory to his ascending the mountain of the Lord and being initiated into the heavenly secrets. According to the ancient traditions, these secrets centered in his being shown the destiny of the universe and having the mysteries of the creation explained to him.

Again the tradition seems in close harmony with the scriptures of the restoration in which we are told that the greater priesthood holds the "key of the mysteries of the kingdom, even the key of the knowledge of God. Therefore, in the ordinances thereof, the power of godliness is manifest. And without the ordinances thereof, and the authority of the priesthood, the power of godliness is not manifest unto men in the flesh; for without this no man can see the face of God, even the Father, and live." (D&C 84:19-22.) All of this "Moses plainly taught to the children of Israel in the wilderness." The ancient Jewish writer and philosopher Philo portrayed each Israelite as being "instructed in the holy secrets and accepted for admission to the greatest mysteries."

As every Sunday School attender knows, when Moses descended with the tables of stone upon which the law was written and saw the wickedness of Israel, his "anger waxed hot, and he cast the tables out of his hands, and brake them beneath the mount." (Exodus 32:19.) Later, he was instructed to hew two other tables of stone and again ascend the holy mountain. In this instance the Lord gave him "the law as at the first," but it was the "law of a carnal commandment," the Lord having taken the higher priesthood and its ordinances from Israel generally, though the prophets would still hold it. (JST, Exodus 34:1-2.)

Though Moses had stood in the presence of the Lord and talked to him face to face, even he lost that privilege for a season. Exodus 33:20 records the Lord saying to him, "Thou canst not see my face: for there shall no man see me, and live." From the Joseph Smith Translation we learn why. Restored to its original purity,the text reads: "Thou canst not see my face at this time, lest mine anger be kindled against thee also, and I destroy thee, and thy people; for there shall no man among them see me at this time, and live, for they are exceeding sinful. And no sinful man hath at any time, neither shall there be any sinful man at any time, that shall see my face and live." (JST, Exodus 33:20.) Moses had "sought diligently to sanctify his people that they might behold the face of God; but they hardened their hearts and could not endure his presence; therefore, the Lord in his wrath, for his anger was kindled against them, swore that they should not enter into his rest while in the wilderness, which rest is the fulness of his glory. Therefore, he took Moses out of their midst, and the Holy Priesthood also." (D&C 84:23-25.)

Certainly this stands as a solemn warning to those of our day. If men are not willing to live worthy to receive the higher priesthood, and if both men and women are not willing to sanctify themselves so that they might enter the house of the Lord and enter into his presence, then the fulness of gospel blessings will be lost to them as they were to Israel anciently. Theirs will be a lesser law and a lesser glory. Paul taught this principle with great power when he asked, "Know ye not that ye are the temple of God, and that the Spirit of God dwelleth in you? If any man defile the temple of God, him shall God destroy; for the temple of God is holy, which temple ye are." (1 Corinthians 3:16-17.)

As the Lord will not visit that temple that has been polluted, so the Holy Ghost will not associate with those who have defiled the temple of their bodies. In remarks at the dedication of the Provo Temple, President Joseph Fielding Smith taught that it is not really temples that we dedicate, for temples are merely mortar and stone; it is people that we dedicate or rededicate to the purposes of the Lord. This is not to say there are not holy places, but it is to say that in large measure the spirit that one experiences in such places is the spirit that they bring with them. They can ascend the mountain of the Lord only as far as they have prepared themselves to do so. When the scriptures speak of our standing in holy places in the last days, they have no reference to our crowding all worthy Saints into the temples, but rather to a people whose lives are dedicated to holiness and who will, therefore, be found magnifying their own office and calling, doing their duty in righteousness.

Revelation of All Truth

As we have previously seen, the Lord has promised to "reveal all mysteries" to those who serve him "in righteousness and truth." (D&C 76:5-7.) Among those who have laid claim to this promise was the brother of Jared. Of him Moroni said, "There never were greater things made manifest than those which were made manifest unto the brother of Jared." These things were recorded by Moroni in what we know as the sealed portion of the Book of Mormon. They have been sealed because the Lord commanded that they were not to go to the world "until the day that they [the Gentiles] shall repent of their iniquity, and become clean before the Lord. And in that day that they shall exercise faith in me, saith the Lord, even as the brother of Jared did, that they may become sanctified in me, then will I manifest unto them the things which the brother of Jared saw, even to the unfolding unto them all my revelations, saith Jesus Christ." (Ether 4:4-7.)

We are then told that those who contend against the principle of revelation, or who deny it, shall be accursed. They shall see "no greater thing," Moroni said; or as Nephi put it, "From them that shall say, We have enough, from them shall be taken away even that which they have." (2 Nephi 28:30.) While those who reject revelation will lose the right to it, those who believe and accept are to be rewarded with even greater manifestations. "He that believeth these things which I have spoken, him will I visit with the manifestations of my Spirit, and he shall know and bear record." (Ether 4:11.) Teaching the same principle to Joseph Smith, the Lord said, "Whosoever believeth on my words, them will I visit with the manifestation of my Spirit; and they shall be born of me, even of water and of the Spirit." (D&C 5:16.) Moroni tells us that when we rend the "veil of unbelief," a veil caused by wickedness, hardness of heart, and blindness of mind, "then shall the great and marvelous things which have been hid up from the foundation of the world" be made known to those who call upon the Father in the name of Christ with a broken heart and a contrite spirit. "And then shall my revelations which I have caused to be written by my servant John be unfolded in the eyes of all the people." (Ether 4:15-16.)

To Have the Heavens Opened

The sacred truths of heaven are not granted to men in wickedness or rebellion; they are the reward of obedience and righteousness. In the full sense of the word, righteousness is found only where good works are combined with ritual observance. Good works are as a memorial in heaven; yet they must be sustained with faith in God, with belief in his word, with repentance from sin, and with the ordinance of baptism, if one is to receive the priceless gift of the Holy Ghost and become a companion of the Revelator. Some have been baptized and received the promise of that association without having lived to obtain it; others have lived circumspectly but have refused the ordinance. Neither can receive the promised gift. As exaltation can be found only in the union of the man and the woman, so the promise of the fulness of heavenly treasure is obtained only in the marriage of good works and ritual observance. Even Christ could not fulfill all righteousness without baptism. (2 Nephi 31:5.)

The promise of the mysteries of the kingdom, or the fulness of revelation, comes only after baptism. "If ye will enter in by the way," Nephi testified, "and receive the Holy Ghost, it will show unto you all things what ye should do." (2 Nephi 32:5.) This is the exclusive providence of the worthy citizenry of the earthly kingdom of God—none else can lay claim to it. Only after baptism are we eligible for the blessings associated with the Melchizedek Priesthood. "The power and authority of the higher, or Melchizedek Priesthood, is to hold the keys of all the spiritual blessings of the church—to have the privilege of receiving the mysteries of the kingdom of heaven, to have the heavens opened unto them, to commune with the general assembly and church of the Firstborn, and to enjoy the communion and presence of God the Father, and Jesus the mediator of the new covenant." (D&C 107:18-19.) When the priesthood is fully operating in the life of a man, then the power to rend the heavens or part the veil will also be found. Through revelation Joseph Smith taught us that "the rights of the priesthood are inseparably connected with the powers of heaven," but he warned that "the powers of heaven cannot be controlled nor handled only upon the principles of righteousness. That they may be conferred upon us, it is true; but when we undertake to cover our sins, or to gratify our pride, our vain ambition, or to exercise control or dominion or compulsion upon the souls of the children of men, in any degree of unrighteousness, behold, the heavens withdraw themselves; the Spirit of the Lord is grieved; and when it is withdrawn, Amen to the priesthood or the authority of that man." (D&C 121:36-37.)

God is known and revelations are received through

the priesthood. It is through the priesthood that the
Holy Ghost, through whom all things may be revealed, is
given. And it is at the hands of the priesthood that all
other ordinances are performed, including all the blessings of the temple, for it is "in the ordinances" that "the
power of godliness is manifest." (D&C 84:20.)

"Draw near unto me and I will draw near unto you,"
the Lord has said. "And if your eye be single to my glory,
your whole bodies shall be filled with light, and there
shall be no darkness in you; and that body which is filled
with light comprehendeth all things. Therefore, sanctify
yourselves that your minds become single to God, and
the days will come that you shall see him; for he will unveil his face unto you, and it shall be in his own time, and
in his own way, and according to his own will." And thus
the instruction, "Prepare yourselves, and sanctify yourselves; yea, purify your hearts, and cleanse your hands
and your feet before me, that I may make you clean; that
I may testify unto your Father, and your God, and my
God, that you are clean from the blood of this wicked
generation." (D&C 88:63, 67-68, 74-75.)

Such was the preparation made by Moses to stand in
the presence of the Lord, and such is the preparation he
sought to have Israel make anciently and that our
prophets seek to have us make today. It is in such preparation that one is endowed with both power and knowledge from on high.

Chapter Four

Seeking Revelation

No man can receive the Holy Ghost without receiving revelations. The Holy Ghost is a revelator. (Joseph Smith, HC 6:58.)

The things of the Spirit can be understood only in the language of the Spirit. In this chapter we will identify those principles which, when properly understood, will make us more fluent in speaking and understanding that language. Ten such principles will be discussed with appropriate scriptural illustrations and texts.

1. Scriptural Study

We are expected to be serious students of the scriptures. Once the Lord has revealed a principle, it is hardly our right to seek to have him repeat it again and again for our gratification and convenience and thus reinforce and reward our spiritual indolence. Those who have little interest in and pay virtually no attention to what God has already said are certainly not in a position to seek further instruction from him. Of those who are slow to listen, the scriptures say the Lord will be slow to hear. (D&C 101:7.) Scolding the Church for their negligence in scriptural study, the Lord said, "Your minds in times past have been darkened because of unbelief, and because you have treated lightly the things you have received—which vanity and unbelief have brought the whole church under condemnation. And this condemnation resteth upon the children of Zion, even all. And they shall remain under this condemnation until they repent and remember the new covenant, even the Book of Mormon and the former commandments which I have given them, not only to say, but to do according to that which I have written—that they may bring forth fruit meet for their Father's kingdom; otherwise there remaineth a scourge and judgment to be poured out upon the children of Zion." (D&C 84:54-58.)

Many, if not most, of the founding revelations of our dispensation were born of scriptural study. It was the text in James that led Joseph Smith to what we now know as the Sacred Grove and his divine appointment with the Father and the Son. It was the pondering of Book of Mormon passages about baptism that led Joseph Smith and Oliver Cowdery to the banks of the Susquehanna River, where their imploring of the heavens was answered by John the Baptist and the restoration of the Aaronic Priesthood. It was concern over a text in the Gospel of John (D&C 76:15) that resulted in our receiving the greatest revelation of our and perhaps of any dispensation—the revelation on the degrees of glory. "I sat in my room pondering over the scriptures," wrote Joseph F. Smith, as he described the circumstances that called forth the great revelation on the redemption of the dead. (D&C 138:1-2, 11.) Again and again the principle has proven itself: nothing is more effective in prompting the spirit of revelation than the study of revelation. "Those who study, ponder, and pray about the scriptures, seeking to understand their deep and hidden meanings, receive from time to time great outpourings of light and knowledge from the Holy Spirit." (McConkie, "Holy Writ: Published Anew," p. 1.)

2. Get the Spirit

The Holy Ghost should be our companion in prayer. He it is who translates the deep and inexpressible feelings of our souls into the language of heaven. He it is who directs our thoughts to those things which in priority we ought to be praying about. It takes the Spirit to get the Spirit, and it takes revelation to get revelation. "He that asketh in the Spirit asketh according to the will of God," Joseph Smith was told, "wherefore it is done even as he asketh." (D&C 46:30.) The apostle Paul taught that the Spirit would strengthen us in our weaknesses, teach us that for which we ought to pray, and, as Joseph Smith paraphrased it, make "intercessions for us with striving which cannot be expressed." (Romans 8:26; HC 5:264.)

Proper prayer is always inspired prayer. The scriptures, teaching us the manner of such prayers, say, "It shall be given you what you shall ask." (D&C 50:30.) Perhaps the perfect illustration of this principle for our day is the prayer offered by President Kimball in the Salt Lake Temple on June 1, 1978. It was this prayer, dictated by the Holy Ghost, that brought forth the revelation extending the priesthood and all of its blessings to worthy males of all nations and races. (*Priesthood,* Deseret Book, 1981, p. 133.) It is the Spirit that attracts the Spirit.

3. The Agency Principle

"It is not meet that I should command in all things," the Lord declared, "for he that is compelled in all things, the same is a slothful and not a wise servant; wherefore he receiveth no reward. Verily I say, men should be anxiously engaged in a good cause, and do many things of their own free will, and bring to pass much righteousness; for the power is in them, wherein they are agents unto themselves. And inasmuch as men do good they shall in nowise lose their reward. But he that doeth not anything until he is commanded, and receiveth a commandment with doubtful heart, and keepeth it with slothfulness, the same is damned." (D&C 58:26-29.)

The quest for the spirit of revelation will find the honest seeker in the position of seeking direction from the Lord on occasion without receiving either a feeling of assurance and confirmation or a feeling of uncertainty, or, in the scriptural phrase, a "stupor of thought." What does one do when no clear answer comes? The principle involved might best be illustrated by the parent/child relationship. Wise parents neither seek nor desire to make every decision for their children. Rather, they teach them correct principles and carefully grant them the freedom to grow to maturity and accountability. This can happen only when the parents are willing to step back and allow their children responsibility in the decision-making process. So it is with our Father in heaven. It is not his desire or purpose to command or compel in all things, but rather to teach us, his children, correct principles so that we might learn to govern ourselves in wisdom and righteousness. It is inevitable that we will find ourselves in situations in which we desire to have him make decisions for us that appropriately we ought to make for ourselves. In such situations, when we pray, no clear yes or no will be forthcoming from the heavens. Since indecision constitutes a decision, we are obligated to make a choice and follow it. In these instances, we make the best decisions we can and put them into operation. This is done in the confidence that if the decision is not right—if there are things unknown to us that would make it seriously harmful—the Lord will intervene and make that plain to us. On the other hand, if our course is appropriate we can anticipate that at some future point, after we have demonstrated our independent judgment, the confirmation will come. In some quiet manner the Lord will manifest his approval.

Developing this same concept, Elder Richard Scott of the First Quorum of Seventy suggests this illustration: "One day a very close friend came to my home. He was a bishop very much enjoying his calling. He had an opportunity for employment in another part of the country and was undecided about whether or not to go. We discussed the principles just reviewed. He went home and made a decision to move. He felt no confirmation of the correctness of that decision, but moved to the new job anyway. His employment was good and his family comfortable, yet he continued to feel somewhat ill at ease, not knowing for sure whether he had made the right decision. A week passed, then a month, then additional months. One day one of the Brethren was assigned to reorganize the stake in the area where he now lived. He received his confirmation from the Lord when he was selected to be the new stake president." (*BYU Speech of the Year*, 1978, p. 102.)

In contrast, consider this experience. A young woman received a proposal from a fine young man she had been dating. Uncertain in her feelings and unable to identify a clear spiritual direction, she sought counsel with her bishop. He explained that he could not and would not attempt to make that decision for her, but suggested that if she committed herself to a course of action, she would almost immediately find it confirmed or hedged up with feelings of foreboding. She went back to the young man and told him that she would marry him. With that commitment came a feeling as though she had been immersed in a sea of darkness. The engagement lasted twenty-four hours. She later suggested that she could not conceive a more dramatic or emphatic answer to her prayers and that she was extremely grateful for it, notwithstanding the temporary embarrassment associated with it.

We would all like to receive an unmistakable spiritual assurance in every major decision that we make, not realizing that if such were always our experience, we would have little opportunity to exercise faith and develop our own spiritual muscles. If I suggest to young people that the perfect assurance that they have married the right person will not come until some considerable time after they have been married, they immediately object to the idea. If, on the other hand, I tell them that the

only way they can know with perfect assurance that the
Church is true, and that baptism brings a cleansing from
sin, is to get baptized and join the Church, they all agree.
We would not expect a perfect testimony of the Word of
Wisdom or the law of tithing without living the principles
involved. Many like illustrations could be cited, but even
at this point it is clear that the perfect testimony of any
principle can be had only after our commitment to it and
after we have begun to live it. The scriptural injunction is
that "ye receive no witness until after the trial of your
faith." (Ether 12:6.)

Living by the Spirit requires the exercise of faith and
agency. It necessitates our standing on our own feet
spiritually, and it often calls for us to make decisions, de-
pending on the Lord to affirm or correct us as may be
necessary. Sometimes to get the Spirit we need to get
moving. This was Nephi's philosophy as he went back to
Jerusalem to obtain the plates of brass. He said, "I was led
by the Spirit, not knowing beforehand the things which I
should do." (1 Nephi 4:6.) Peter followed the same pattern. After he had received the dream of the clean and
unclean animals, he "doubted in himself what this vision
which he had seen should mean," but he accepted the invitation of the servants of Cornelius and went to
Caesarea with them. It was only after he had gone and
while he taught those assembled in Cornelius's home that
the Holy Ghost fell on him and gave him the meaning of
the vision. It was then that he was able to say, "Of a truth I
perceive that God is no respecter of persons: but in every
nation he that feareth him, and worketh righteousness, is
accepted with him." (Acts 10:17, 34-35.) In this instance,
Peter's answer did not come as he knelt in prayer a
the rooftop in Joppa; rather, it came as he stood on his
feet in the line of his duty in Caesarea.

4. The Right Reason
Wilford Woodruff said that a member of the
Quorum of the Twelve told him that he had prayed for

many years to enjoy the administration of an angel but that his prayers had never been answered. "I said to him," Elder Woodruff recounted, "that if he were to pray a thousand years to the God of Israel for that gift, it would not be granted, unless the Lord had a motive in sending an angel to him. I told him that the Lord never did nor never will send an angel to anybody merely to gratify the desire of the individual to see an angel. If the Lord sends an angel to anyone, He sends him to perform a work that cannot be performed only by the administration of an angel." (*Deseret Weekly* 53:642-643.) Proper prayer must always be appended to proper reason. "Ye ask, and receive not," wrote the apostle James, "because ye ask amiss, that ye may consume it upon your lusts." (James 4:3.) Teaching that concept anew in our dispensation, the Lord has instructed us to seek earnestly after the best spiritual gifts, warning also against the spirit of sign seekers, who, he said, "consume it upon their lusts." (D&C 46:9.) The warning is that we do not pray for that which will gratify our appetites but rather for those things of lasting worth.

As to sign seekers the Lord said, "He that seeketh signs shall see signs, but not unto salvation. Verily, I say unto you, there are those among you who seek signs, and there have been such even from the beginning; but, behold, faith cometh not by signs, but signs follow those that believe. Yea, signs come by faith, not by the will of men, nor as they please, but by the will of God. Yea, signs come by faith, unto mighty works, for without faith no man pleaseth God; and with whom God is angry he is not well pleased; wherefore, unto such he showeth no signs, only in wrath unto their condemnation." (D&C 63:7-11.) Those who testify that they have been saved because they have had, as they suppose, some marvelous spiritual experience have been seduced by evil spirits and doctrines of devils. Salvation comes by obedience to the laws and ordinances of the gospel, not by marvelous spiritual experiences. Reminding Joseph Smith of this principle, the Lord said, "Although a man may have many revelations, and have power to do many mighty works, yet if he boasts in his own strength, and sets at naught the counsels of God, and follows after the dictates of his own will and carnal desires, he must fall and incur the vengeance of a just God upon him." (D&C 3:4.)

Joseph Smith taught us that it was a "great thing to inquire at the hands of God, or to come into His presence; and we feel fearful to approach Him on subjects that are of little or no consequence, to satisfy the queries of individuals." (HC 1:339.) Further, we have been warned that we are not to trifle with sacred things (D&C 6:12) and that we are not to ask for those things which we "ought not" (D&C 8:10). That which has been properly sought will be given "that is expedient for you; and if ye ask anything that is not expedient for you, it shall turn unto your condemnation." (D&C 88:64-65.)

Though we are invited to freely seek of the heavens, we are to do so with some restraint. The divine privilege is not to be abused; that which is sacred is to be treated sacredly, and that which is of most worth is to be treated with utmost care. We are to seek only that which is proper and needful, that which is to our blessing and which will enable us to more effectively bless others.

5. Heed and Diligence

Revelation is granted in proportion to the preparation we have made to receive it. Joseph Smith said, "I could explain a hundred fold more than I ever have of the glories of the kingdoms manifested to me in the vision, were I permitted, and were the people prepared to receive them. The Lord deals with this people as a tender parent with a child, communicating light and intelligence and the knowledge of his ways as they can bear it." (HC 5:402.) All experienced gospel teachers have learned, as the Prophet said, that they can teach only to the extent that their pupils are prepared to learn. So it is when we seek instruction of the Spirit. We can be taught only in relation to the preparation that we have made to understand. We learn only in relation to what we know.

Alma taught this principle: "It is given unto many to know the mysteries of God; nevertheless they are laid under a strict command that they shall not impart only according to the portion of his word which he doth grant unto the children of men, according to the heed and diligence which they give unto him. And therefore, he that will harden his heart, the same receiveth the lesser portion of the word; and he that will not harden his heart, to him is given the greater portion of the word, until it is given unto him to know the mysteries of God until he knows them in full. And they that will harden their hearts, to them is given the lesser portion of the word until they know nothing concerning his mysteries; and then they are taken captive by the devil, and led by his will down to destruction. Now this is what is meant by the chains of hell." (Alma 12:9-11.) Alma also taught that this principle was as true of nations as it was of individuals. He said, "The Lord doth grant unto all nations, of their own nation and tongue, to teach his word, yea, in wisdom, all that he seeth fit that they should have." (Alma 29:8.)

Brigham Young, illustrating the limitations we place on the Spirit of the Lord, said, "I do not even believe that there is a single revelation, among the many God has given to the Church, that is perfect in its fulness. The revelations of God contain correct doctrine and principle, so far as they go; but it is impossible for the poor, weak, low, grovelling, sinful inhabitants of the earth to receive a revelation from the Almighty in all its perfections. He has to speak to us in a manner to meet the extent of our capacities." President Young then used as his illustration the efforts of the Saints to teach the Lamanites, pointing out that they had to speak in a language that the Indians could understand before they could teach them principles that would lift and exalt them.

Continuing, he said, "You have to use the words they use, and address them in a manner to meet their capacities, in order to give them the knowledge you have to bestow. If an angel should come into this congregation, or visit any individual of it, and use the language he uses in heaven, what would we be benefitted? Not any, because we could not understand a word he said. When angels come to visit mortals, they have to condescend to and assume, more or less, the condition of mortals, they have to descend to our capacities in order to communicate with us. I make these remarks to show you that the kingdom of heaven is not yet complete upon the earth. Why? Because the people are not prepared to receive it in its completeness, for they are not complete or perfect themselves.

"The laws that the Lord has given are not fully perfect, because the people could not receive them in their perfect fulness; but they can receive a little here and a little there, a little today and a little tomorrow, a little more next week, and a little more in advance of that next year, if they make a wise improvement upon every little they receive; if they do not, they are left in the shade, and the light which the Lord reveals will appear darkness to them, and the kingdom of heaven will travel on and leave them groping. Hence, if we wish to act upon the fulness of the knowledge that the Lord designs to reveal, little by little, to the inhabitants of the earth, we must improve upon every little as it is revealed." (*Journal of Discourses* [JD] 2:314.)

6. Revelation Comes Line upon Line

As President Young indicated, it is in the accumulation of spiritual experiences that the knowledge of salvation comes. The supposition that through a particular experience, or that at some specific time, one obtains sal-

43

vation demeans both God and man. It debases God in
granting the glories of eternity so cheaply, and it denies
the divine nature of man in not requiring more of him. If
it is foolishness to suppose that an earthly education
could come from the experience of a moment, how much
greater the foolishness to suppose that the education
necessary for eternity could be had so easily. Even Christ
"received not of the fulness at first, but continued from
grace to grace, until he received a fulness." (D&C 93:13.)
The Saints have been promised "revelations in their
time," but only as they prove themselves "faithful and
diligent." (D&C 59:4.) The knowledge of heaven is obtained "line upon line, precept upon precept, here a little
and there a little." (2 Nephi 28:30.) All are directed to
seek understanding of eternal things through study and
by faith. All must "grow up" in faith, seeking that time
when they can "receive a fulness of the Holy Ghost."
(D&C 109:14-15.) It is intended that our association with
the Holy Ghost grow deeper and richer with the passing
of years.

7. The Right Time

Abraham was sixty-two years of age when he received
the promise of the Lord that he would be the father of a
great nation. (Abraham 2:14.) He and Sarah had already
been childless in marriage for some years. Nearly four
decades were to pass before Sarah, at the age of ninety,
and Abraham, then one hundred years of age, would become the parents of Isaac, the child of the promise. One
can only wonder at the thoughts of their hearts and the
anguish of their souls as they waited on the Lord for the
fulfillment of that promise. Enough of the story has been
preserved that we know of the difficulty of that struggle.
During those long years of waiting we find Abraham
going before the Lord and suggesting that the promise
be filled in the steward of his house, a slave, who would be
his lawful heir should he have no children. The Lord re-

sponded: "This shall not be thine heir; but he that shall come forth out of thine own bowels shall be thine heir." (Genesis 15:3-4.) Then we find Sarah granting to Abraham her handmaid as a second wife so that perhaps he might have seed by her. This Abraham did, and in his eighty-sixth year Ishmael was born of the bondswoman Hagar. Again we find Abraham appealing to the Lord to grant the promise to Ishmael, and again the Lord refused. Abraham was told that the child must be of him and Sarah. (Genesis 17:19-21.) Then came the three holy men to assure Abraham that he and Sarah were to give birth to a son. Sarah, standing in the doorway of the tent, overheard the conversation and laughed within herself, for she had long since passed the years of childbearing. The Lord spoke to Abraham, saying, "Wherefore did Sarah laugh, saying, "Shall I of a surety bear a child, which am old? Is any thing too hard for the Lord?" (Genesis 18:9-14.)

It is at the discretion of God that all heavenly gifts are granted. The scriptures promise a time when he will "unveil his face," but they also remind that "it shall be in his own time, and in his own way, and according to his own will." (D&C 88:68.) Alma identified diligence, patience, and long-suffering as the companions of revelation. (Alma 32:43.) James, before inviting all who lacked wisdom to ask of God, counseled, "Let patience have her perfect work, that ye may be perfect and entire, wanting nothing." (James 1:4.) To those of our day, the Lord has said that through humility we will gain strength and then will be "blessed from on high, and receive knowledge from time to time." (D&C 1:28.) It is for the Lord, in his wisdom, to choose when and how he will speak.

In a discussion with a group of unwed mothers on getting answers to prayers, someone asked, "When can we expect an answer?" The implications of the question were obvious. Each had sinned, each had done that which was grievously offensive to the Spirit, yet they were repentant. They wanted to do what was right, and they wanted the Lord's help as they attempted to do it. In response, it was suggested that they consider the promise of the Lord in the revelation on spiritual gifts. There the Lord extends the promise of those gifts to those who keep *all* his commandments, and to those who "seeketh so to do." (D&C 46:9.) It is in that phrase "seeketh so to do" that those of us who are something short of perfection find solace and encouragement. The promise of spiritual direction is granted to all who sincerely seek that direction. Perfection, or even near perfection, is not the prerequisite for the blessings of heaven. The Lord is not blind to even the humblest of efforts on the part of those who seek him in sincerity and truth. Yet we can fully expect his response to come "in his own time, and in his own way, and according to his own will." It is not for us to dictate terms or establish deadlines for the Lord.

8. Priesthood Channels

In our brief discussion of the forms of revelation in chapter 2, we considered the concept of stewardship, the essence of the principle being that our right to revelation is confined to our personal stewardships. No one is entitled to revelation for those who preside over them. We now return to that principle to emphasize those stewardships or priesthood channels as a primary source of personal revelation. The conversion of Paul constitutes a classical illustration. It was while Paul was journeying to Damascus that the Lord finally got his attention. This personal confrontation with the Lord, who appeared in his glory, found Paul quite teachable. Trembling and astonished, with a humility he had never before known, Paul asked the Lord, "What wilt thou have me to do?" The answer given is marvelously significant. He was instructed to go into Damascus and wait. Then the Lord directed Ananias, a local priesthood leader, to go to Paul, restore his sight, teach him the gospel, and baptize him.

(Acts 9:1-18.) Ananias had already been given the responsibility in that part of the Lord's kingdom to bless by the power of the priesthood, teach the gospel, and baptize. He had every answer that Paul needed, and it was from him that Paul must get it, if the Lord's house was to remain a house of order. So it was in the Sacred Grove, when the youthful Joseph Smith asked the Father which of all the churches he should join. The Father, who had chosen his Firstborn to rule and reign as our Savior and King, pointed to him, saying, *"This is My Beloved Son. Hear Him!"* (JS–H 1:17.) As Christ would not assume the stewardship of Ananias, so the Father would not assume the office he had given his Beloved Son. Similarly, when an angel visited Cornelius, he neither taught nor baptized him. Rather, he instructed Cornelius to send for Peter, from whom he would obtain the mind and will of the Lord; at Peter's feet he would be taught and at Peter's hands he would be baptized and receive the gift of the Holy Ghost. (Acts 10.)

The concept of stewardship and channels is clearly one to which God and angels give allegiance. A principle so reverenced in heaven can hardly be taken lightly on earth. There are blessings, revelations, and ordinances that can be received only at the hands of those appointed to grant them. To refuse to recognize those sources is to refuse those blessings.

9. Sacred Silence

In the holy union of man and woman, that which they share together can only be profaned by sharing with others. So it is with the things of the Spirit. There are experiences that are of such a high spiritual nature that they are not "lawful for man to utter." (D&C 76:115.) Let us call this the doctrine of sacred silence. Bluntly stated, the doctrine is that the Lord will not reveal himself to blabbermouths.

In teaching the gospel, we have been warned not to

"cast pearls before swine." In our prayers, our preaching, and our hymns, we have been cautioned to avoid the too frequent use of the name of Deity. "Your minds in times past have been darkened because of unbelief," the Lord told the early Saints, "and because you have treated lightly the things you have received." (D&C 84:54.) The wise and proper use of spiritual experiences is the prerequisite for the continued receipt of the same. Patriarchal blessings are an example. The blessing by the patriarch is a personal revelation. The intent of such blessings is personal consolation, not public communication. They are for the individual and, as appropriate, for his family. Under most circumstances they are not a proper source for a Sunday School lesson or sacrament meeting talk. "Remember," the Lord said, "that that which cometh from above is sacred, and must be spoken with care, and by constraint of the Spirit." (D&C 63:64.) "Let us be faithful and silent," Joseph Smith said, "and if God gives you a manifestation, keep it to yourselves." (HC 2:309.)

10. Revelation Begets Revelation

All things produce after their own kind. Doubt begets doubt, while the offspring of faith and belief are in their image and likeness. "Intelligence cleaveth unto intelligence; wisdom receiveth wisdom; truth embraceth truth; virtue loveth virtue; light cleaveth unto light; mercy hath compassion on mercy and claimeth her own; justice continueth its course and claimeth its own." (D&C 88:40.) Thus it is that revelation begets revelation.

It is expected that we do more than read of spiritual feasts that were eaten anciently; we too must approach the table and feed our souls. The tree of life continues to bring forth living fruit. To have one revelation is to have the seedlings of yet others. Again the scriptures declare, "That which is of God is light; and he that receiveth light, and continueth in God, receiveth more light; and that

light groweth brighter and brighter until the perfect
day." (D&C 50:24.) Among the Saints, revelation is a
habit, and so it must be, for "from them that shall say, We
have enough, from them shall be taken away even that
which they have." (2 Nephi 28:30.)

Chapter Five

A Personal Urim and Thummim

God hath not revealed anything to Joseph, but what he will make known unto the Twelve and even the least Saint may know all things as fast as he is able to bear them. (Joseph Smith, in The Words of Joseph Smith, *p. 4.)*

God has granted to righteous people from time to time certain divinely appointed devices to facilitate the receipt of revelation. Among them have been the Urim and Thummim, seer stones, and the Liahona. Those who mock the true order of God have had their own forms of these divinely appointed instruments. This system of counterfeits, which is known as divination, has included the throwing of sticks or arrows into the air (Ezekiel 21:21); examination of the liver or other organs of an animal (Ezekiel 21:21); teraphim, which are small idols representing household gods (1 Samuel 19:13, 16; Judges 17:5); necromancy, or communication with the dead (Deuteronomy 18:11; 1 Samuel 28:8); astrology, or reading the stars (Isaiah 47:13; Jeremiah 10:2); and hydromancy, or divination with water, done either by noting the reflections or inducing a trance by this means (Genesis 44:5, 15). The Saints have been commanded to avoid divination in all its forms. (Deuteronomy 18:9-12.) Yet what of those devices which enjoy divine favor? What right do the Saints have to draw upon their powers for personal use? In seeking an answer to such questions, we turn to the wise counsel given by a prophet father to an inquiring son.

A Personal Liahona

Helaman, the son of Alma the younger, understood that God was no respecter of persons. He knew that if God were to be just, he could not grant certain favors to one that under similar circumstances he would not grant to all. Yet the justice of God is not always immediately apparent. Now, to those familiar with the inquiring minds of youth, it is an easy matter to imagine the questions with which the young Helaman challenged his father. Why had they not received a Liahona, as had Lehi and his family? Were they not as worthy? Did not God love them as well? Or had God lost his power to aid men as he had done anciently?

With wisdom and patience, Alma responded. He explained that "Liahona," by interpretation, means compass. "The Lord prepared it," he said, ". . . to show unto our fathers the course which they should travel in the wilderness. And it did work for them according to their faith in God; therefore, if they had faith to believe that God could cause that those spindles should point the way they should go, behold, it was done; therefore they had this miracle, and also many other miracles wrought by the power of God, day by day." (Alma 37:38-40.) Alma explained that because these miracles were worked by such natural means, Lehi and his family took them for granted. They ceased to be faithful and diligent, and thus their divine compass ceased to work. They found themselves wandering in the wilderness and unable to find food or water. Finally their afflictions brought humility; they returned to their knees, and their prayers rekindled their faith. With the return of their faith, the Liahona commenced again to work for them.

According to Alma, this was a temporal story intended to illustrate a spiritual truth. It was a way of dramatizing that it is as easy for those of all ages "to give heed to the word of Christ," which will point them in a straight course, one that leads to eternal life, as it was for father Lehi and his family to give heed to those same principles and make the Liahona work. (Alma 37:42-44.) Thus Alma showed his son that faith and diligence were required of Lehi's family in the same manner that they are required of all families if they are to follow a divinely approved course. The "work of Christ" was to Helaman as it is to all, a personal compass, or Liahona. Revelation is available to every man and his family, but it is granted only according to the faith and diligence they exercise in that which they have already been given.

Types and Shadows

Alma's explanation of the workings of the Liahona brings the story of the Book of Mormon into focus. Alma called it a "type" and a "shadow." Types and shadows are events of the past that constitute a prophetic replica of events in the future. Alma felt that Lehi's story was universal. He saw it as a miniature of the past that, when the light of the gospel fell on it, cast a prophetic shadow to the future, a shadow that would be in its own image and likeness. Let us consider the story and the shadow it cast.

Lehi and his family were living near the great city of Jerusalem. The nation of the Jews were in apostasy, ripe in iniquity, yet as is always the case with such people, they made great professions to righteousness. To such, Jerusalem was not just the center of the world, it was the spiritual capital. The Lord told Lehi that if he and his family were to escape the destruction that was to come upon their nation, they must abandon it. Leaving wealth and comfort and trusting solely in the Lord, the family began their great journey in faith. All ideas that the journey would be easy because the Lord looked after them were quickly dispelled. Yet, as a manifestation of his love,

the Lord gave them the Liahona, the divine compass, to
show them their way. The Liahona served as a constant
reminder that the watchful eye of the Lord was over
them and that he alone could direct their course. It
worked, as we have been told, according to their diligence and faith. Because of the simplicity of the way,
they became spiritually careless, even slothful, and the
compass ceased to work. Now they wandered in circles,
lost in the wilderness, afflicted with hunger and thirst.
Realizing that they had brought this plight upon themselves, Lehi and his family sought the Lord in humility
and prayer. Having witnessed their renewed desire to
serve the Lord faithfully, the compass began once again
to point a straight course for them. Thus they were led to
their land of promise and blessed beyond all expecta-
tions.

The story is universal. All men find themselves in a
world professing righteousness while reveling in wickedness, a world from which they and their families must
flee if they are to be saved from the inevitable bondage
and enslavement of sin. To do so, they must trust in the
Lord, leaving behind worldly wealth and honors. The
journey is long and hard, but if they are faithful, the
Lord will show them the way. Should they cease their diligence, they will cease following a straight course and will
find themselves wandering in the wilderness of life, afflicted with all manner of troubles. Yet, if they return to
the Lord, he will return to them; and eventually they will
inherit a land of eternal promise with blessings and
wealth beyond what they could ever have imagined.

The Word of Christ: A Spiritual Compass

There is no divine compass, no Urim and Thummim,
no seer stone, no revelatory device of any kind that will
operate independent of faith and righteousness. The ancient tradition was that the Urim and Thummim would
work only for a high priest filled with the Holy Spirit. To

the unworthy "the stones withheld their power" while
the worthy "received an answer to every inquiry." (Louis
Ginzberg, *The Legends of the Jews* 3:172-73.) When Saul,
who had been disobedient, inquired of the Lord, "the
Lord answered him not, neither by dreams, nor by Urim,
nor by prophets." (1 Samuel 28:6.) Nowhere is this principle better taught than in our present illustration, as
Alma teaches Helaman that "it is as easy to give heed to
the word of Christ, which will point to you the straight
course to eternal bliss, as it was for our fathers to give
heed to this compass, which would point unto them a
straight course to the promised land." (Alma 37:44.)
Nephi's testimony was that the words of Christ "will tell
you all things what ye should do." (2 Nephi 32:3.)

Gospel covenants constitute one of the important
ways that the word of Christ acts as a personal Liahona or
compass. In baptism we promise to take upon ourselves
the name of Christ and to stand as witnesses of him "at all
times and in all things, and in all places . . . even until
death." (Mosiah 18:9.) Certainly this is a constant guide
to our behavior. It is in the honoring of this covenant that
we receive the promise of the companionship of the Holy
Ghost. In like manner the Melchizedek Priesthood
comes with an oath and covenant. The oath is on God's
part as he promises us the fulness of eternal blessings if
we will but keep our covenant to magnify our office and
callings and sustain those called to preside over us in the
priesthood. (D&C 84:33-40.) In the temple endowment
we covenant to be clean and chaste, to be charitable, and
to consecrate all of our means, our time, and our talent to
sustaining the cause of the gospel. This covenant is called
an endowment, because through our being true to it we
are "endowed with power from on high." (D&C 38:32;
43:16.) In the sacred vows of celestial marriage we
further covenant to pursue a course of fidelity to family
and God. The living of such covenants with exactness
and honor assures that we could not get seriously lost in

the wilderness of life. These covenants do not contain answers to all of life's challenges and problems, but they establish a sure course and constitute the prerequisite for
additional light and direction as it is necessary. It is in the
ordinances that the "power of godliness is manifest."
(D&C 84:20.)

As only the power of obedience and righteousness
could make the Liahona work, so it is with the word of
Christ: the Bible directs a straight course only to the obedient and righteous. Satan too quotes scripture. Many di-
vergent paths are marked with scriptural references. As
there was more than one city named Enoch and more
than one people professing to be the sons and daughters
of God anciently, so it is today. Judaism, Christianity, and
Islam all claim Abraham as their father, and all profess to
be the children of the Book. Yet only to those obedient to
its laws and ordinances and those seeking so to do will it
point a sure course.

Such was the experience of Joseph Smith and Oliver
Cowdery. Describing the restoration of the Aaronic
Priesthood and the ordinance of baptism under the
hands of John the Baptist, Joseph Smith said: "Immediately on our coming up out of the water after we
had been baptized, we experienced great and glorious
blessings from our Heavenly Father. . . . We were filled
with the Holy Ghost, and rejoiced in the God of our salvation. Our minds being now enlightened, we began to
have the scriptures laid open to our understandings, and
the true meaning and intention of their more mysterious
passages revealed unto us in a manner which we never
could attain to previously, nor ever before had thought
of." (JS–H 1:73-74.)

Unfolding the Mysteries

Obviously, not all see the same thing when they read
the same scriptural passages. Some see only that which
they want to see; all see only what their preparation al-

lows them to see. In the context of our story, Alma shows his son what he had failed to see, that is, how the story of Lehi and his family casts a shadow that can easily be likened to circumstances that are the common lot of all the saints. It is in making such inspired applications that we breathe the breath of life into the written word. Could it be that in the divine providence of things, virtually every story that has been preserved for us in the scriptures has hidden within itself its own types and shadows, types and shadows that are in some instances prophetic while others contain counsel and instruction of great importance to us today? Let us illustrate using first an Old Testament story that contains a Messianic prophecy.

Our story is that of the prophet Samuel, who was told by the Lord to cease mourning over the disobedience of King Saul and to anoint another as king of Israel. Samuel was directed to take his horn of oil and go to Jesse the Bethlehemite, for it would be among Jesse's sons that the Lord would choose a king. Dutifully Samuel went to Bethlehem and sought out Jesse. There Jesse was instructed to sanctify his sons and to bring them before Samuel. When Jesse's first son, Eliab, was brought before Samuel, he said, "Surely the Lord's anointed is before him," for Eliab apparently looked every inch a king. But the Lord got a hold of Samuel and said, "I have refused him: for the Lord seeth not as man seeth; for man looketh on the outward appearance, but the Lord looketh on the heart." One by one Jesse brought seven of his sons before Samuel, yet none was chosen of the Lord. Dismayed, Samuel asked Jesse if those were all of his sons, and Jesse reluctantly confessed that there was one other, one of whom perhaps they were a little embarrassed and whom they had left to tend the sheep. "Send and fetch him," said Samuel, "for we will not sit down till he come hither." When the young shepherd boy, David, was brought into the presence of Samuel, the Lord said, "Arise, anoint him: for this is he." (1 Samuel 16:1-12.)

Surely this story stood for all of Israel as a prophetic type announcing the manner in which their promised Messiah would come. Consider the shadow that it cast. Would not the promised Messiah also be found in Bethlehem? Would he not be the son of Jesse? Would he not be the overlooked one, the obscure one, but nonetheless the Good Shepherd? Would he not come while all of Israel was looking for a king—a king of temporal power and grace? And had not the Lord rejected such and sent to Israel one whose power was not at that time to be temporal but spiritual? And would he not bear the name David, an honored Hebrew name meaning "beloved" or "well-beloved" son? And was he not to be, as was David of old, the Lord's anointed? The English word *Christ* comes from a Greek word meaning anointed and is the equivalent of *Messiah,* which is the same as the Hebrew anointed. Thus, when David was anointed as king of Israel, it was to be understood that he was to be a type of Israel's ultimate King, the Christ.

The shadows cast by the stories of the scriptures can be both prophetic and instructional. As an illustration, consider the story of Moses and the spies he sent into the land of Canaan. Moses formed the group by choosing one of the chief rulers from each of the tribes. Oshea of the tribe of Ephraim was apparently designated to be their leader. Not satisfied with Oshea's name, however, Moses changed it to Joshua. (Numbers 13:16.) Now, we are left to ask, is there something of purpose in all of this for our day? Let us consider the implication of Moses' choosing twelve men who were the "heads of the children of Israel" (Numbers 13:3) to act as guides to show Israel the way from their wilderness wanderings to their promised land, and in doing so, setting one at their head and specifying that he is to be called Joshua. Let it not be lost upon the reader that Joshua is the Hebrew form of the name Jesus. Are we not to see in this a deliberate attempt to say to Israel in all future generations that the only way they can escape the wilderness of life and obtain the eternal inheritance promised them is to follow Jesus and the Twelve?

And what of the scriptural stories of our own dispensation—are they not also intended to cast a shadow from the image of which all truth seekers can find instruction? Let our example be the Joseph Smith story as it is found in our modern scripture. Our story is an account of a young man struggling with the promptings of the Spirit and seeking to know which of all the churches he should join. In doing so, he finds himself overwhelmed with the "war of words" and the "tumult of opinions" with which the world is filled. He finds himself asking, "What is to be done? Who of all these parties are right; or, are they all wrong together? If any one of them be right, which is it, and how shall I know it?" (JS–H 1:10.)

In this struggle he learns two great lessons. First, he learns that the various denominations of his day interpreted the scriptures so differently "as to destroy all confidence in settling the question by an appeal to the Bible." (JS–H 1:12.) Second, he learns that an answer, if one is to be found, can come only from actually doing what the Bible directs—ask of God. In his attempt to do this he is resisted, even threatened with destruction, by a power from the unseen world. He is then freed from that power of darkness by a light that gradually descends upon him; and in the midst of this light, which continuously grows brighter, he finds God and receives the instructions he seeks. He is warned not to join with the creeds and churches of the world, for they "teach for doctrines the commandments of men, having a form of godliness, but they deny the power thereof." (JS–H 1:19.) He receives much that he cannot express to others and is promised additional instruction in the future. When he tries to share this experience with those who should be most ready to accept and rejoice in it, he finds himself both rebuked and rejected, and he becomes an object of scorn.

Are such experiences peculiar to Joseph Smith, or are they in many points universal to all who honestly seek after truth? Do they not contain within them the outline of virtually every conversion story that the reader has heard?

The Past Is the Prophecy of the Future

Much that is in the revelations of the past is but the prophecy of the future. A classic example of this is found in the Joseph Smith Translation of Christ's discourse on the Mount of Olives in which He spoke of the signs of the times. His disciples came to him asking what signs would foreshadow the destruction of the temple and the nation of the Jews. They also asked what signs would fore-shadow the end of the world and the destruction of the wicked. Significantly the answer to both questions was the same, notwithstanding the fact that two thousand years separated the two events. Here we see the genius of the scriptures. The destruction of the temple and a wicked nation in the meridian of time are but the pre-figuring, or the prophetic replica, of the same cycle of events that are to take place in the last days. Hence, the better we understand the meridian events, the better we are prepared to understand the events of the last days. The past becomes the key to the present and the future.

Nor is this an isolated principle. In this same dis-course, Christ prophetically announced that "as it was in the days of Noah, so it shall be also at the coming of the Son of Man; for it shall be with them, as it was in the days which were before the flood; for until the day that Noah entered into the ark they were eating and drinking, marrying and giving in marriage; and knew not until the flood came, and took them all away; so shall also the coming of the Son of Man be." (Joseph Smith–Matthew 1:41-43.)

This principle directed the writing of the Book of Mormon. Unlike the Bible, the Book of Mormon was written exclusively to those of our day. It is not a volume of scripture that was had in the homes and churches of the Book of Mormon peoples. Rather it is an abridgment of many scriptural records kept by the ancient inhabitants of this land, an abridgment made under the direction of the Spirit to specifically draw from their history those events which would find a ready application in our day and to sustain those illustrations with doctrines that are eternal. "Behold," Moroni testified as he aided in the writing of this book, "I speak unto you as if ye were present, and yet ye are not. But behold, Jesus Christ hath shown you unto me, and I know your doings." (Mormon 8:35.)

The Spirit Is Forever the Same

When they are studied under the direction of the Spirit, there is a timelessness about the scriptures as there is about the principles they teach. As Lehi declared, "The Spirit is the same, yesterday, today, and forever." (2 Nephi 2:4.) And as Nephi testified, those who have entered into covenants with the Lord must then "press forward with a steadfastness in Christ, having a perfect brightness of hope, and a love of God and of all men. Wherefore, if ye shall press forward, feasting upon the word of Christ, and endure to the end, behold, thus saith the Father: Ye shall have eternal life." (2 Nephi 31:20.)

We must assume that if seer stones were as readily available as the scriptures, they too would be found covered with dust on many bookshelves, for there are no shortcuts to divine favor or the knowledge of the heavens.

Chapter Six

Understanding Personal Revelation

By learning the Spirit of God and understanding it, you may grow into the principle of revelation, until you become perfect in Christ Jesus. (Joseph Smith, HC 3:381.)

It is one thing to have a revelation and entirely another to understand it. Indeed, revelation is misunderstood more often than it is understood. "Why then," one might ask, "would God give it? Surely he would not give a revelation if it were not going to be understood." To respond to such questions, we turn to the Bible, our textbook on revelation. In fact, the Bible itself is the perfect illustration of the principle. The world is full of people professing to believe the revelations of the Bible, while at the same time disagreeing on virtually every doctrine found between its covers. Obviously it is one thing to have the Bible and entirely another to understand it. More specifically, it is one thing, even among Latter-day Saints, to have the book of Isaiah and entirely another to understand it. And what of the book of Revelation? Who among the best of scriptural scholars and the most spiritually mature profess to fully understand it? Joseph Smith indicated that our inability to fully understand the book of Revelation is quite excusable. He said, "I make this broad declaration, that whenever God gives a vision of an image, or beast, or figure of any kind, He always holds Himself responsible to give a revelation or interpretation of the meaning thereof, otherwise we are not responsible or accountable for our belief in it. Don't be afraid of being damned for not knowing the meaning of a vision or figure, if God has not given a revelation or interpretation of the subject." (HC 5:343.)

It Takes Revelation to Understand Revelation

It takes prophets to understand prophets, revelation to understand revelation, scripture to understand scripture, the Spirit to understand the Spirit. And as Joseph Smith explained, when God does not choose to give a particular interpretation, we are not accountable for it. In the canon of scripture are many revelations that God in his wisdom has not chosen to unfold to us at the present time. As there is a time and a season for all things in the temporal world, so there is also in the realm of spiritual things; and it is for God to determine the times of our understanding.

At this point our questioner might observe that the point is well made as far as institutional revelation is concerned, but he might also remind us that our primary interest at the present moment is with personal revelation. "Are not personal revelations given to be understood by the particular person to whom they are given?"

Since much of the canon of scripture was personal revelation when it was first given, we can turn to it to answer this question. An experience of Joseph Smith provides an interesting case study. "I was once praying very earnestly," he said, "to know the time of the coming of the Son of Man, when I heard a voice repeat the following: Joseph, my son, if thou livest until thou art eighty-five years old, thou shalt see the face of the Son of Man; therefore let this suffice, and trouble me no more on this matter." (D&C 130:14-15.) Here we have a personal revelation given to the most spiritually sensitive and experienced man of our dispensation. At the present time we have no knowledge of any man who received or recorded more prophecy and revelation than did Joseph Smith. In explanation of this experience, he said; "I was left thus, without being able to decide whether this coming referred to the beginning of the millennium or to some previous appearing, or whether I should die and thus see his face." He then added, "I believe the coming of the Son of Man will not be any sooner than that time." (D&C 130:16-17.) Certainly in this instance we can say that it was one thing for Joseph Smith to have a revelation and entirely another for him to understand it. If anything is to be learned from this experience, perhaps it is that if we tease the Lord with questions that we ought not ask, he may taunt us with answers that we cannot understand.

A number of scriptural stories tell of an individual or group that has been granted some form of a heavenly manifestation and has not been able to interpret or understand the message given. Amulek announced with pride that he was the great-grandson of Aminadi, "who interpreted the writing which was upon the wall of the temple, which was written by the finger of God." (Alma 10:2.) The writing was there for all to see, but apparently only Aminadi was able to read it.

In like manner Belshazzar and his thousand lords were unable to read the message written by the fingers of God on his palace wall. Babylon's wisest men were summoned and offered wealth and power if they could interpret the Lord's message to the king, and none were able to do it. The queen reminded Belshazzar that Daniel was a man of great spiritual power, and he was then summoned. Standing before the king, Daniel boldly denounced Belshazzar's sins and then interpreted what astrologers, Chaldeans, and soothsayers could not: that God had numbered the days of Belshazzar's kingdom, and it was now finished. Belshazzar had been weighed in the balance and was found wanting. As the message came from God, so the interpretation need come from him also.

Joseph of Egypt's prisonmates dreamed dreams, but it was to Joseph that they turned for interpretations. Pharaoh's dreams remained a mystery to all the wise men of Egypt, yet God manifested their meaning to Joseph.

Peter taught that "no prophecy of the scripture is of any private interpretation." The prophecy came as holy men were moved upon by the Holy Ghost, he said, and its interpretation must come in the same manner. (2 Peter 1:20-21.) The principle is as true of individual revelation as it is of institutional revelation. Paul taught the same principle, saying, "The things of God knoweth no man, but the Spirit of God. Now we have received, not the spirit of the world, but the spirit which is of God; that we might know the things that are freely given to us from God. Which things also we speak, not in the words which man's wisdom teacheth, but which the Holy Ghost teacheth; comparing spiritual things with spiritual. But the natural man receiveth not the things of the Spirit of God: for they are foolishness unto him: neither can he know them, because they are spiritually discerned." (1 Corinthians 2:11-14.)

Personal Revelation Demands Study

The same effort in study and prayer is necessary to understand personal revelations as is necessary to understand institutional revelation. Unfortunately, many are as indifferent to that effort as they are to the effort necessary to understand the canon of scripture. Yet if the principles are consistent, we would have to say that it is one thing to have a personal revelation, that is, a patriarchal blessing, and entirely another to understand it. Many more patriarchal blessings have been given than have been understood.

When Joseph Smith was translating the Book of Mormon, Oliver Cowdery, who was acting as scribe, sought the privilege of translating. In response to Oliver's request, the Lord granted his desire along with the assurance that he would have the spirit of revelation. Despite this promise, though, Oliver's attempts to translate met with failure. This caused him considerable consternation, in response to which the Lord said: "Do not murmur, my son, for it is wisdom in me that I have dealt with you after this manner. Behold, you have not understood [again we note, it is one thing to have a revelation and entirely another to understand it]; you have supposed that I would give it unto you, when you took no thought save it was to ask me. But, behold, I say unto you, that you must study it out in your mind; then you must ask me if it be right, and if it is right I will cause that your bosom shall burn within you; therefore, you shall feel that it is right. But if it be not right you shall have no such feelings, but you shall have a stupor of thought that shall cause you to forget the thing which is wrong; therefore, you cannot write that which is sacred save it be given you from me." (D&C 9:6-9.)

Oliver's experience is a classic illustration that the revealed promise of success does not excuse one from the responsibility of the work and effort necessary to succeed. The spirit of revelation is a close companion to the spirit of intense study. Such study often results in a sudden stroke of ideas, which Joseph Smith described as "pure intelligence flowing into you." "By learning the Spirit of God and understanding it," he said, "you may grow into the principle of revelation." (HC 3:381.)

Understanding Personal Revelation Requires Faith

The things of the Spirit are to be understood "by study and also by faith." (D&C 88:118.) A power of understanding comes in and through faith that can be had in no other way. The Lord said that he would "give unto the faithful line upon line, precept upon precept; and I will try you and prove you therewith." (D&C 98:12.) The promise is to the "faithful," who are to receive here a little and there a little, but only as they are tried and proven.

Again we can take the canon of scripture as our example of a principle equally true on a personal basis. In writing the Book of Mormon record, Mormon said that he included only the "lesser part" of the teachings of Christ to the Nephite peoples. He said that that lesser portion was to be given to men first "to try their faith," and that only after they had accepted and believed the lesser part would the "greater things be made manifest unto them. And if it so be that they will not believe these things, then shall the greater things be withheld from them, unto their condemnation." Mormon added that he was about to write it all, "but the Lord forbade it, saying: I will try the faith of my people." (3 Nephi 26:8-11.)

Faith is the only currency with purchasing power in heaven. The silver and gold that give this coin its value are study and good works.

We Grow into an Understanding of Personal Revelation

As we grow into our understanding of the scriptures, so we should grow into our understanding of personal revelation. The understanding we have of a patriarchal blessing, given during our teenage years should be greatly exceeded by the understanding we have of the same blessing in mature adult years. Alma, in his great discourse on faith, indicated that we cannot know the things of the Spirit with perfect surety at first. (Alma 32:26.) Spiritual light dawns gradually.

As a young man, Nephi was caught away in the Spirit unto an exceeding high mountain, where he was shown a great vision. He saw Mary and the birth of Christ; he saw the ministry of Christ even to his being lifted upon the cross. He saw that the world would reject Him and his gospel. Nephi witnessed the visit of Christ to the Nephites, their age of glory, and their eventual apostasy.

He saw the spirit of darkness sweep throughout the lands of Europe through the influence of a great and abominable church. He saw how Columbus was worked upon by the Spirit and led to cross the ocean. He saw those who would follow in pursuit of religious freedom and of their great war with their mother nation. He saw the marvelous influence that the Bible would have in the new world and then witnessed the coming forth of the Book of Mormon and the restoration of the gospel. He saw the events of earth's history even up to the destruction of the great and abominable church, including things that he was forbidden to write, for they were yet to be written by the apostle John. (1 Nephi 11–14.) Now, might we say that it was one thing for Nephi to see this marvelous vision and quite another for him to fully understand it? Thus we find him saying, "My soul delighteth in the things of the Lord; and my heart pondereth continually upon the things which I have seen and heard." (2 Nephi 4:16.)

Heavenly truths are to be constantly pondered. The divine injunction is: "Thou shalt teach them diligently unto thy children, and shalt talk of them when thou sittest in thine house, and when thou walkest by the way, and when thou liest down, and when thou riseth up." (Deuteronomy 6:7.) Such is the very system of revelation. We are to treasure up in our minds "continually the words of life," thereby gaining the promise that "it shall be given [us] in the very hour" that which we need. (D&C 84:85.) "Yea, behold, I will tell you in your mind and in your heart, by the Holy Ghost, which shall come upon you and which shall dwell in your heart. Now, behold, this is the spirit of revelation." (D&C 8:2-3.)

All Who Will Hear May Hear

Though they endlessly asked questions of Christ, the Pharisees and Sadducees were not listening with an honest ear to the answers that were given. It is difficult to conceive a more marvelous opportunity lost. They prided themselves in their knowledge of the scriptures, yet failed to understand their meaning. "Search the scriptures," Christ challenged them, "for in them ye think ye have eternal life: and they are they which testify of me." (John 5:39.) All are invited to ask of God, but it need be remembered that it is "counted evil unto a man, if he shall pray and not with real intent of heart; yea, and it profiteth him nothing, for God receiveth none such." (Moroni 7:9.)

Elder Boyd K. Packer of the Council of the Twelve relates a story that illustrates this point. Years ago as the naturalist John Burroughs was walking through a park on a summer evening, he heard a bird sing, despite all the noise of city life. "He stopped and listened! Those with him had not heard it. He looked around. No one else had noticed it. It bothered him that everyone should miss something so beautiful. He took a coin from his pocket and flipped it into the air. It struck the pavement with a ring, no louder than the song of the bird. Everyone turned; they could hear that!" (*Conference Report*, October 1979, p. 27.) We hear what we train our minds to hear.

During those years of small children, Elder Packer and his wife divided the children into "his" and "hers" for night tending. Sister Packer would get up with the new baby, and Elder Packer would get up for the one cutting teeth. "One day," Elder Packer remembers, "we came to realize that each would hear only the one to which we were assigned, and would sleep very soundly through the cries of the others." (Ibid., p. 28.) Again, we hear what we train our minds to hear.

Often the whisperings of the Spirit go unheard because we are too busy to listen. President David O. McKay often illustrated this principle with an experience from the life of John Wells, who years before had served in the Presiding Bishopric. "A son of Bishop Wells was killed in Emigration Canyon on a railroad track. Brother

John Wells was a great detail man and prepared many of the reports we are following up now. His boy was run over by a freight train. Sister Wells was inconsolable. She mourned during the three days prior to the funeral, received no comfort at the funeral, and was in a rather serious state of mind. One day soon after the funeral service while she was lying on her bed relaxed, still mourning, she says that her son appeared to her and said, 'Mother, do not mourn, do not cry. I am all right.' He told her that she did not understand how the accident happened and explained that he had given the signal to the engineer to move on, and then made the usual effort to catch the railing on the freight train, but as he attempted to do so his foot caught on a root and he failed to catch the hand rail, and his body fell under the train. It was clearly an accident. Now listen. He said that as soon as he realized that he was in another environment he tried to see his father, but he couldn't reach him. His father was so busy with the duties in his office he could not respond to his call. Therefore, he had to come to his mother. He said to her, 'You tell father that all is well with me, and I want you not to mourn anymore.'" (Related by Harold B. Lee to seminary and institute faculty, July 6, 1956.)

The revelations of heaven are given in such a manner that all who will hear may hear (D&C 1:11), while those who choose not to hear will not hear (Alma 10:6). When the voice of the Father spoke from the heavens testifying that Jesus was the Christ, some said that it only thundered, others that an angel spake; but John, who had ears to hear, recorded the words of the Father. (John 12:28-29.) Emphasizing the need for listening ears, President Spencer W. Kimball observed that "it is usually through another person that he [God] meets our needs." (*Ensign*, December 1974, p. 5.) President J. Reuben Clark said, "We do not lack a prophet; what we lack is a listening ear by the people and a determination to live as God has commanded." (*Conference Report,* October 1948, p. 82.)

In the Lord's kingdom there are no positions of presidency without counselors. Be it remembered that Joseph Smith turned to his brother Hyrum as he weighed the choice to flee or to cross the river to Nauvoo, a decision that led to Carthage and martyrdom. "Brother Hyrum," he said, "you are the oldest, what shall we do?" (HC 6:549.)

To Understand with the Heart

President Harold B. Lee frequently said that "when your heart begins to tell you things that your mind does not know, then you are getting the Spirit of the Lord." (*New Era,* February 1971, p. 3.) The antithesis is also true. Nephi lamented that his brothers "were past feeling," that they were so hard of heart they could not "feel his words." (1 Nephi 17:45.) To explain why he veiled gospel truths in parables, Christ said: "For this people's heart is waxed gross, and their ears are dull of hearing, and their eyes they have closed; lest at any time they should see with their eyes, and hear with their ears, and should understand with their heart, and should be converted, and I should heal them." (Matthew 13:15.) As we have already noted, the revelations of heaven speak to both the heart and the mind of man. (D&C 8:2.) The phrases "filled with joy," "peace of conscience," "much assurance," "peace to your mind," "confidence wax strong," "heart burn within," "bosom shall burn," and "feel that it is right" constitute the scriptural language describing the spirit of revelation. All true religious experiences will embrace such feelings, for as Joseph Smith put it, truth "tastes good." (HC 6:312.)

The Principles Are Constant

If one must study, pray, and obey to understand institutional revelation, then one must study, pray, and obey to understand personal revelation. There is a constancy in gospel principles, for "the Spirit is the same, yesterday, today, and forever." (2 Nephi 2:4.) And as the Spirit is the same, the principles that attract it are the same. There is a direct and inseparable relationship between our ability to understand institutional revelation and our ability to understand personal revelation. If we are familiar with the voice that is speaking in the scriptures, we will recognize that voice when it speaks to us. It is a familiarity with that voice that we seek. Thus the scriptures become our guide or textbook to understanding personal revelation. This being the case, the reader is now invited to give attention to the questions of how and why each of the standard works came into being and the role that each of them is ordained to play in facilitating our understanding and receipt of personal revelation.

Chapter Seven

A Bible! A Bible!

But thus saith the Lord God: O fools, they shall have a Bible; and it shall proceed forth from the Jews, mine ancient covenant people. And what thank they the Jews for the Bible which they receive from them? Yea, what do the Gentiles mean? Do they remember the travails, and the labors, and the pains of the Jews, and their diligence unto me, in bringing forth salvation unto the Gentiles? (2 Nephi 29:4.)

The Bible has the distinction of being the world's best-known and least-understood book. Judaism, Christianity, and Islam all claim Bible traditions for their beliefs. The word *bible* is a derivation of the Greek *biblia*, which means "the books." The Bible is a compilation of sacred books, a divine library. There is no universal agreement as to which books rightfully ought to be a part of this sacred collection. The Samaritans admit only the Pentateuch (the five books of Moses) to their Bible library, the Jews accept the books of the Old Testament, the Christian world adds the twenty-seven books of the New Testament, and the Roman Catholics add still another fifteen books, known as the Apocrypha, written during the two centuries before Christ.

Had we lived in Bible times, we would not have made the mistake of thinking of the Bible as a single book, simply because it never existed in that form. Anciently, books were written on scrolls; during Old Testament times they were made of skins, while in New Testament times they were made of papyrus. The Bible that Jesus knew (the Old Testament) consisted of from twelve to twenty scrolls of different lengths. Had they been united into one scroll, they would have been too large and heavy to use. Books in leaf form did not emerge until about the second century; and printed books as we know them, not until the sixteenth century.

So the Old Testament as we know it was not known to the Jews anciently. The books that constitute the Old Testament were written on separate rolls or scrolls, one containing the Pentateuch; another, Isaiah; another, the Prophets; another, the Psalms, and so on even to the inclusion of books or scrolls that are now lost to us. Obviously, there could be no particular order or sequence to the Old Testament library—this would come only after they were printed in book form. The scriptures as found in the arks of Jewish synagogues even today are scrolls, not the leaf-bound books like the one being read. Understanding the nature of the ancient scriptural books can be important in interpreting their message. For instance, John the Revelator wrote in what is now the last chapter of our Bible that no one was to add to the words of "this book." (Revelation 22:18.) Some have attempted to apply John's statement to the entire Bible, using it as an argument against the possibility of future revelation. John, however, was not writing the final chapter in a then existent book; he was writing on a scroll separate and apart from the other books that had been or yet would be written—books that eventually became the Bible. The compilation of these scrolls into book form did not take place until hundreds of years after his writing.

It is interesting and important to have some idea of how the Bible evolved to its present form. In question and answer form, let us briefly tell that story.

1. When and how did the Bible come into being?

Until the printed book emerged, the Bible did not exist in one volume. The earliest we know of the New Testament existing as the collection of books recognized today is A.D. 367. No member of the church organized by Christ in the meridian of time ever read it! The apostasy was complete before it existed.

The center of synagogue worship was the reading of scripture. That is what the service existed for. When it was no longer possible for the followers of Christ to worship in the synagogues of the Jews, they met as they could to read the scriptures and to partake of the sacrament. It was the Old Testament that was read each Sunday in these meetings. The Old Testament scriptures constituted Christ's Bible. He fed his own soul along with the souls of his disciples on it. When Christ appeared to his disciples in the upper room after his resurrection, he impressed on them the fact that all that had happened to him was in exact accord with the prophecies in the "law of Moses, and in the prophets, and in the psalms." (Luke 24:44.) Not only does such a statement confirm the inspiration of the Old Testament writings, but it also affirms that they have been divinely approved and are to be regarded as canonical. In their missionary work and teaching, Christ and his disciples quoted constantly from the Old Testament canon.

Yet by our standards the ancients had very limited access to the scriptural records. It appears, at least in one instance, that significant portions of the scriptural records were lost to the house of Israel when the Israelites chose to wander in darkness. After two wicked kings, Josiah ascended to the throne, and in his eagerness to restore the worship of Jehovah, he directed that the temple be renovated. While this was being done, the book of the law was found. A priest took it to Josiah, who joyfully received it and set about putting its teachings once again into effect. (2 Kings 22, 23.) He put a stop to the idolatrous practices of the day, ordered the offerings of sacrifice to be confined to the city of Jerusalem, and required the Passover celebration to be held there.

This story certainly appears to be an Old Testament figure or type announcing to all generations that idolatrous practices will result in the loss of the word of the Lord and proper religious worship, while zeal in righteousness will bring forth the word again from its place of hiding.

Among Latter-day Saints, the best-known story to illustrate the limited access the ancients had to the scriptural records and the difficulty they had in obtaining them is the struggle of Nephi and his brothers when they were sent by their father to get the brass plates from Laban. These plates contained a record comparable to the Old Testament down to that time. That these records were not readily available (at least on metal) is certainly evidenced by the jealousy with which Laban guarded them and the fact that it became necessary for Nephi and his brothers to take his life in order to obtain them.

Among Old Testament prophets, Ezra is known as the second Moses, because of his efforts to reintroduce the "law" to the nation of Israel. After having brought Judah back to the land of Judea following their seventy years in Babylonian captivity, he caused that they should gather together to have the scriptures read to them. A platform was built for him to stand upon so that the people could see and hear as he read from the sacred scroll. "And Ezra the priest brought the law before the congregation both men and women, and all that could hear with understanding, upon the first day of the seventh month. And he read . . . from the morning until the mid-day." In reverence to the law, the people stood as he read; and since his people had acquired the language of Babylon and generations had grown up not knowing the rites and ordinances of the gospel, Ezra translated as he read, and the sense and meaning were explained. The people wept as the scriptures were unfolded to them.

This may have been the first time in their lives that they had heard the scriptures read and explained. They would have fasted and stood, and wept the more, but Ezra declared the occasion to be one of celebration, not mourning, so they celebrated and came each day for seven days until all the law had been read and explained to them. (Nehemiah 8.)

To the Bible of Jesus' day have been added twenty-seven documents—four Gospels, one book of church history, twenty-one letters, and a book of visions. By what authority and by what reason was the collection made? If Jesus of Nazareth was the Christ, as he and his followers testified on countless occasions, then his words and other inspired declarations about him and his doctrines can be no less authoritative than those of the prophets who taught in his name and prophesied of him in Old Testament times. The Old Testament record centers in him. The written account of his words and those who taught with the same inspiration and authority as did the Old Testament prophets must therefore be regarded with at least the same veneration as that which he himself accorded to the Old Testament oracles.

As to how this collection of writings came into being, it appears that most or perhaps even all of the letters of Paul were written before any of the rest of the New Testament. Scholars date them as having been written between the years A.D. 49 and 62. One evidence that Paul's letters preceded the other writings of the New Testament is that none of those sources are quoted by Paul (although he does refer to specific teachings of Jesus). Had such sources been available to him, he most certainly would have quoted them. His letters were, of course, handwritten (there being no such thing as printing), and there is no reason to suppose that he would have made but a single copy of them. With the exception of the book of Hebrews, they were written to correct or instruct in some local situation where he had labored or desired to

labor as a missionary. These were letters in the very real
sense of the term. They were not prepared for publication nor with the idea that they would be included in a
book, which, in the lifetime of Paul, they were not.

The commission given by Christ to his disciples to
teach the principles of his gospel to those of every nation
was not limited to oral preachment; it also embraced the
written word. The earliest of meridian documents were
letters; these were followed by the Gospels or testimonies
of his special witnesses. Nothing in any of these writings
is not present at least in principle in what Jesus himself
taught. Their authors were his ambassadors; their words
were his words; their doctrines were his doctrines. All
that the disciples did was done in his name. They did not
add to his gospel. Rather, under the direction of the
Spirit that he promised to them, they interpreted and ap-
plied it. Their voice became his voice and was so regarded by the community of believers. Thus, long before
such teaching or testimony was gathered into book form,
it was regarded as authoritative. No formal gathering of
the saints ever voted to canonize the books of the New
Testament, but because of their authoritative nature and
the respect with which the authors were regarded, tradition accomplished what the government of the church
never survived to do.

The first of the Gospels to be written was apparently
Mark's. His Gospel, which was greatly influenced by his
companionship with Peter, is believed to have been written in Rome sometime around A.D. 65 to 70. Shortly
thereafter Matthew wrote his Gospel, obviously writing
to his Hebrew brothers who professed to be waiting for
the coming of Messiah. Luke, the companion of Paul in
much of his missionary work, was next to write, writing
both the book that bears his name and its sequel, the book
of Acts. The last of the Gospels written was John's. In his
Gospel, he emphasized events and doctrines not mentioned by the other Gospel writers. The Gospels were not

intended to be biographies of the Savior. They are testimonies of his divine sonship, his works, and his doctrines. Sometime after having written his Gospel, John wrote the Apocalypse, or book of Revelation, as it is more commonly known.

So the tradition evolved of reading New Testament books in worship services along with the books of the Old Testament. Considerable struggle was yet ahead before it would be determined which books would constitute the canon of scripture and which would not. Eusebius of Caesarea (A.D. 270-330), the great church historian, divided the books into three classes—those universally accepted, the disputed books, and the spurious ones. Those he felt to be universally accepted were the Four Gospels, the Letters of Paul, 1 John, and 1 Peter. The Apocalypse hovered between being universally accepted and being disputed. The disputed books were James, Jude, 2 Peter, and 2 and 3 John, though many regarded James to be spurious. Among the books that eventually lost favor or general acceptance were the Epistle of Barnabas, the Teachings of the Twelve Apostles, and the Shepherd of Hermas.

The first known list of the twenty-seven books that we recognize appeared in a letter written by the bishop of Alexandria to the churches announcing the date of Easter in A.D. 367. At this point the canon was regarded as complete and closed. Thus, the collection of books constituting the New Testament library was determined some considerable time after the apostasy of the meridian church was complete.

2. How and why was it determined that no other books could be added to the New Testament library?

The manner in which the New Testament evolved created the question as to whether the canon was at some point to be closed, and if so, how the quota of sacred books was to be determined. No book in the Bible indicated a time when revelation and the writing of scripture

should cease. In fact, quite to the contrary, many passages of scripture indicated that this was not to be the
case. Strangely enough, it was these very promises that
brought the canon to a close. On the eve of his crucifixion, the Savior told his disciples that he had many things
to teach them, but that they could not bear them at that
time. He then promised that the Holy Ghost would guide
them "into all truth" and show them "things to come."
(John 16:12-14.) Toward the end of the second century,
after spiritual gifts and revelation had ceased, a man
called Montanus came on the scene denouncing the
existing apostasy. He announced himself to be the Advocate promised by the Savior and said that he had come to
give them the promised revelation. The church solved
the problem of dealing with such heretics by announcing
that the revelations of God had been given and that the
canon of scripture was closed. From then on, they determined the Spirit was to be confined to aiding men in understanding and applying what had already been written, but no new revelation was to be given.

3. *What does the term "testament" mean, and how do the Old
and New Testaments differ in respect to that meaning?*

The Bible is divided into two unequal parts, respec-
tively known as the Old Testament and the New Testament. The names are something of misnomers and as
such have led to considerable misunderstanding in the
world and even some confusion in the Church. The common sense in which the word *testament* is used in English
is in reference to someone's last will and testament. As
used to divide the two major portions of the Bible, no
such meaning is intended. A more descriptive word, and
one that more accurately represents in English the
thought desired to be conveyed, is *covenant.* Modern
translations of the Bible consistently use *covenant* in pref-
erence to the King James use of *testament.* The inconsis-
tency of the translators in the King James Bible is easily
seen by comparing Hebrews 9:19-20 with Exodus 24:8.

In both instances an account is being given of Moses sacrificing various animals as a token of the blood of Christ. The New Testament has Moses saying, "This is the blood of the testament which God hath enjoined unto you," while the Old Testament uses the more correct and descriptive word *covenant.* We could then, quite properly, replace the word *testament* with the word *covenant* in the titles of the two parts of the Bible.

A covenant is a mutual promise between God and an individual or a group of chosen people. Still, even the titles Old Covenant and New Covenant are not entirely suitable for describing the differences between the two major divisions of the Bible. The idea conveyed by such usage is that the thirty-nine books of the Old Testament are descriptive of the carnal law, the schoolmaster, or lesser law, while the New Testament deals with Christ's introduction for the first time of a higher law. Yet in fact, for the greater part of the time period of the Old Testament (approximately twenty-five hundred years), the period from Adam to Moses, the higher law existed. From father Adam to the time of Moses, the Lord's people had the fullness of the gospel of Jesus Christ. It was only from Moses to Christ, a period of approximately fifteen hundred years, that the Mosaic or lesser law was had. Christ was not introducing the gospel for the first time; rather, he was restoring the gospel known to righteous people in "Old Testament" times.

The provisions of the Mosaic law were understood to be temporary and had not always existed. This is plainly taught in the revelations of the restoration and is evident in a careful reading of the New Testament. For instance, in his discourse on marriage, Christ observed that the Mosaic law allowed divorce and remarriage because of the hardness of men's hearts, but he said that "from the beginning it was not so." (Matthew 19:8-9.) Paul, who tells us that there is but one gospel (Galatians 1:9), also testified that Abraham had that gospel and was approved of the Lord 430 years before Moses was given the lesser law (Galatians 3:8-18).

4. *Did the ancient Bible library contain books that are now lost to it?*

Yes. The Book of Mormon not only tells us that "many plain and precious things" have been taken from the Bible, but it also identifies a number of them. Among them are the writings of Zenock, Zenos, and Neum. (1 Nephi 19:10; Jacob 5; 3 Nephi 10:16.) Lehi also quoted extensively from a prophecy of Joseph of Egypt (2 Nephi 3) that has been lost from Bible manuscripts, though it has been restored in the Joseph Smith Translation (JST Genesis 50:24-38). In fact, Joseph of Egypt authored a scriptural record now lost to us. Alluding to this record, Lehi said that Joseph "truly prophesied concerning all his seed. And the prophecies which he wrote, there are not many greater. And he prophesied concerning us, and our future generations; and they are written upon the plates of brass." (2 Nephi 4:2.) The Book of Mormon also contains a prophecy of Joseph's father, Jacob, that is not found in the Bible. (Alma 46:24-26.)

Within the Bible are a good number of references to books considered by the Bible writers to be scripture but that are now lost to it. For instance, in 1 Chronicles 29:29 we read: "Now the acts of David the king, first and last, behold, they are written in the book of Samuel the seer, and in the book of Nathan the prophet, and in the book of Gad the seer." Other like references include these: book of the Wars of the Lord (Numbers 21:14); book of Jasher (Joshua 10:13); book of the acts of Solomon (1 Kings 11:41); prophecy of Ahijah (2 Chronicles 9:29); book of Shemaiah (2 Chronicles 12:15); book of Jehu (2 Chronicles 20:34); sayings of the seers (2 Chronicles 33:19); an epistle of Paul to the Corinthians, earlier than to our present 1 Corinthians (1 Corinthians 5:9); and the book of Enoch (Jude 1:14).

In addition to the above, there are many instances in

the New Testament when Christ or one of his disciples quoted a scripture familiar to their audience but not now a part of the Old Testament. Christ testified saying, "Abraham rejoiced to see my day: and he saw it, and was glad." (John 8:56.) No record of any such experience on Abraham's part is found in the Old Testament. (Again the record of this event was restored to the Old Testament text by Joseph Smith in the Joseph Smith Translation.) Similarly, Paul in his writings quotes from Genesis about the Melchizedek Priesthood, noting things not in our modern Bibles but restored to the ancient text by Joseph Smith. (Compare Hebrews 7:3 with JST, Genesis 14:28.)

Many like examples could be given, but perhaps none of greater significance than the many instances in which Jesus quoted passages to sustain his claim to be Messiah, passages for which there is no Old Testament counterpart today. Among them were passages indicating that he would be delivered unto the Gentiles, mocked, spit upon, scourged, and resurrected after three days. (Luke 18:31-33; 24:46; John 20:9.) Jesus also testified that the Bible of his day had been tampered with. "Woe unto you, lawyers!" he cried, "for ye have taken away the key of knowledge, the fulness of the scriptures." (JST, Luke 11:53.)

5. *What do we know of ancient writings that once vied for inclusion in the Bible?*

A number of books popularly read in Christian worship services of the second and third century did not survive the scrutiny of time and tradition to find a place in the Bible canon. For that matter, some of the books in our present Bible clung to canonical status only with considerable difficulty. Among those books whose influence was not sufficient to maintain permanent place in the Bible library were the Gospel of Peter, the Shepherd of Hermas, the Letter of Clement of Rome to the Corinthians, and the Letter of Barnabas. The Gospel of Peter apparently once held a place of honor equal to, if not greater than, that accorded to the Four Gospels. It gives an account of the events surrounding the crucifixion of Christ. This account of the crucifixion contains numerous variations of fact with the story as told by the four Gospel writers. (See *The Lost Books of the Bible and the Forgotten Books of Eden,* New York: World Publishing Co., pp. 282-86.)

The Shepherd of Hermas is a visionary allegory that involves two heavenly figures, an old lady and a shepherd, who call Hermas to repent of thoughts he had after seeing a beautiful maiden girl. The work testifies of a God who created all things from nothing. It is clearly an uninspired work.

Clement, a fellow missionary with Paul (Philippians 4:3), wrote his epistle to correct certain dissensions that had arisen among the Corinthian saints. It is an edifying work notwithstanding the fact that as an argument to sustain the reality of the resurrection, Clement uses the fable of the phoenix, a beautiful, lone bird that, according to Egyptian mythology, lived in the Arabian desert for five or six hundred years and then consumed itself in fire, rising renewed from the ashes to start another life.

In like manner, the letter of Barnabas is an interesting work with appropriate instruction that slips below the level of a canonical work when Barnabas, in an explanation of the clean and unclean animals of the Mosaic Law, says such things as, "The hare every year multiplies the places of its conception," and the hyena changes "its kind, and is sometimes male and sometimes female."

6. *What are the Apocrypha books of the Catholic Bible, and how reliable are they?*

By popular usage, a collection of fifteen books from the intertestamental period, now a part of the Catholic Bible, are known as the Apocrypha. However, since Catholic theology regards them as scripture, the Catholics do not refer to them by this name. Why these books have been designated as "apocrypha" is unclear. In modern usage the word is most often used to label a story as fictitious. Such is not the true meaning of the word. Etymologically, apocrypha means secret or hidden. Advocates of these books maintain that their contents were to be kept secret or hidden from unbelievers or those not worthy to receive the sacred truths they contained. The opponents of these books have argued that they ought to be hidden because they are spurious and heretical.

These books were a part of the Septuagint Bible, the Greek translation of the Old Testament made for Jews living in Alexandria, Egypt, during the last three centuries before Christ. The Jews of Palestine limited the contents of their scripture to the books we know as the Old Testament. (The Apocrypha books are listed and summarized in the dictionary of the new Latter-day Saint edition of the Bible. See pages 610-11.)

The Apocrypha form an invaluable link between the Old and New Testament periods. As to their doctrinal value, the Roman Catholic church has accepted them, at least in part, because it finds in them some justification for masses for the dead and the dogma of purgatory. The Protestant world has rejected them, at least in part, because of their strong emphasis on salvation by works. Significantly, none of the authors of the books of the New Testament quote from these books, while they frequently quote from most of the thirty-nine books of Hebrew canon of the Old Testament.

Since the Apocrypha were a part of the Bible Joseph Smith was using while doing the work we know as the Joseph Smith Translation, he inquired of the Lord about them. He was told many things in them were true and that they had mostly been translated correctly. However, he was cautioned that there were also many things in them that were not true, resulting from changes in the texts made by later scribes, and that it was therefore not necessary for him to translate the Apocrypha. (D&C 91.)

7. Will other books yet be added to the Bible?

From the revelations available to us, it is evident that more scriptural records have been lost than preserved. The time will come when these records will be had again among the faithful Saints. Reference is made in the Doctrine and Covenants to a parchment made and hidden by John the Revelator. This writing contains the promise Jesus gave him that he would "tarry" until the Second Coming in order that he might "prophesy before nations, kindreds, tongues and people." (D&C 7.) Another revelation promises the restoration of the full account of what took place on the mount of transfiguration. (D&C 63:20-21.) A Gospel written by John, presumably the Baptist, is also promised (D&C 93:18) along with the book of Enoch (D&C 107:57), which contains the prophecies of Adam that extend to the end of the earth's history. The Book of Mormon tells us that we will yet have the records of the Lost Tribes. (2 Nephi 29:13.) And, of course, we will yet have that portion of the Book of Mormon which was sealed in which is found "a revelation from God, from the beginning of the world to the ending thereof." (2 Nephi 27:7, 10, 22.)

8. Do the Dead Sea Scrolls have anything to do with the Bible records?

Yes. Until 1947, when the Dead Sea Scrolls were found, the oldest extant manuscript copies of the Hebrew Scriptures came from the ninth and tenth centuries A.D. In the caves of Qumran, near the shores of the Dead Sea, was found a library of religious books dating back to the second century before Christ. Thus this remarkable find provided copies of at least fragments of all Old Testament books (except Esther) that were almost a thousand years older than the extant manuscripts. While these texts sustained the hope of scholars that only minor changes had been made in Bible manuscripts through that period, other records found among this desert community indicated that they had many practices thought in the sectarian world to be original with the church Christ organized in the meridian of time. Since this find, scholars have concluded that Christ borrowed many of his teachings and doctrines from these peoples. Latter-day Saints, for whom it is common knowledge that the gospel was had in its fulness in many dispensations before Christ, can only be amused at the surprise manifest by the so-called Christian world at such a find.

9. *In what language were the teachings of the Bible originally given?*

Since Bible history spans four thousand years, the original language in which its teachings were given is varied. Father Adam, the first author of a scriptural record, wrote in a language that was "pure and undefiled," known to us as the Adamic or celestial language. It appears that the Jaredites retained that tongue and recorded their scriptures in it. (Ether 12:24-25.) It is doubtful, however, that Adam's writings and those of Enoch and the other ancient patriarchs were available to Moses in the Adamic when he wrote the book of Genesis. Like the Prophet Joseph Smith, Moses could have had the original content of those writings revealed to him without ever possessing the texts upon which they were written. The original language from which the Old Testament books have come to us is Hebrew, though the apostles often quoted from the Greek translations in their teachings.

The language in which Jesus and the apostles taught would have been Aramaic among themselves and in addressing the people of Judea or Galilee. They would have used Greek in addressing strangers. Greek was the universal language of the day and would have been understood and spoken by many in Palestine, but the language of the people was a dialect of the ancient Hebrew, the Western or Palestinian Aramaic. As Edersheim notes, "A Jewish Messiah who would urge His claim upon Israel in Greek, seems almost a contradiction in terms." (Alfred Edersheim, *The Life and Times of Jesus the*

Messiah, New York: Longmans, Green and Co., 1927, 1:129-30.) As far as the New Testament is concerned, it is highly likely that we do not possess a single saying of the Savior in the language in which he spoke it. The New Testament comes to us from Greek manuscripts, so what we have is a translation of a translation of the original language in which Christ taught.

10. *Do any of the original manuscripts from which the Bible came still exist?*

No. As already noted, we were no closer to an original text of the Old Testament than the ninth or tenth century A.D. before the discovery of the Dead Sea Scrolls. The Dead Sea scrolls give us manuscripts that are nearly a thousand years older but that are still hundreds and thousands of years removed from the original manuscripts. One of the difficulties here was the custom of the Jews to destroy old manuscripts when new texts had been made from them. As to the New Testament, no manuscripts are dated earlier than the first half of the second century (A.D. 150). Most of the New Testament manuscripts are only fragments. Our present New Testament has come from the painstaking effort of scholars to piece together the fragments of some five thousand manuscripts. These five thousand manuscripts contain an estimated 400,000 textual variations. Of the thousands of Old and New Testament manuscripts that have survived, no two of them are precisely alike.

11. *When was the Bible first translated?*

The first translation of the Hebrew Bible (Old Testament) was begun in Alexandria, Egypt, in the mid-third century B.C. Since the rising generation of Jews no longer understood their mother tongue, a Greek translation was necessary. The resultant translation is known as the Septuagint, because according to legend it was the work of seventy scholars, six from each of the twelve tribes, all of whom produced identical versions in seventy days. In fact, more than two centuries were necessary to complete the work.

The Septuagint (LXX) was extremely influential among Jews living outside Palestine and became the Bible of the early Greek-speaking Christians. Thus the Bible, which to this time had been the exclusive providence of the Hebrew race, was able to be taken to peoples of all the known world. Most of the Old Testament passages cited in the New Testament are either direct quotations or paraphrases of the Septuagint Bible. Indeed, so completely did Christians take over this Jewish translation that the Jews were forced to produce another version for their own use. This new version differed from the original; whereas the Hebrew Bible has twenty-four books, the Septuagint has thirty-nine books plus the Apocrypha. In the Hebrew, Samuel, Kings, and Chronicles each represent one book. In the Septuagint, they are divided into two books each. In the Hebrew, Ezra and Nehemiah form one book, as do the Twelve Minor Prophets. In the Septuagint, they are classified separately. Omitting the Apocrypha, our Bibles follow the order of the Septuagint.

The next great step in the story of Bible translations took place between A.D. 385 and 405 when St. Jerome produced the Latin Vulgate under the direction of the Bishop of Rome. This made the scriptures, both Old and New Testaments, available to educate clergy in the Roman Catholic Church. No other major translation was made for nearly a thousand years. Pre-Reformation translators merely rendered Jerome's Latin into the languages of modern Europe. Not until William Tyndale in the 1500s was a translation made again from the Hebrew and Greek manuscripts.

12. *How did we get our modern English translation of the Bible?*

For more than a thousand years Jerome's Latin Bible

was the parent of every version of the scriptures produced in Western Europe. The Catholic council of Trent
in 1546 announced it to be the authentic version and decreed that no one should dare to reject it under any pre-
text whatever. Yet during that period Latin had become
a dead language and the Bible could only be read by a
few of the clergy and some scholars. Still the tradition
held that Latin was the divine language. The Catholic
worship service did not center in preaching or reading
the word of God from the Bible; rather, the emphasis
was on the sacrifice of the mass. With the service in Latin,
its emphasis was ceremonial rather than informational.
The Bible and its teachings were virtually unknown to
the people. It was said of the church of that day that
"scarcely anything but the mere name of Christ remained; His true doctrine being as far unknown to the
most part, as His name was common to all." (John Foxe,
Foxe's Christian Martyrs of the World, Chicago: Moody
Press, p. 321.)

Thus the stage was set for a courageous scholar by the
name of John Wycliffe to give to English-speaking
people a Bible they could read. Excommunicated from
the church of Rome for his opposition to pardons, in-
dulgences, and masses for the soul, Wycliffe secreted
himself from his enemies and translated the Vulgate into
English. Wycliffe died before his enemies could make a
martyr of him; yet forty years after his death his bones
were dug up, burned, and the ashes flung into a river.

The greatest weakness in Wycliff's Bible was that it so
faithfully reproduced Jerome's Latin Vulgate into English that every error of the Vulgate was perpetuated.
Still it was the first great step in getting the Bible into the
hands of the common man. Despite the fact that it had to
be written longhand, a task that would take a copyist ten
months, it was widely scattered throughout England. As
might be imagined, the cost was such that only the weal-
thy could afford it, but they seemed to be free in letting

others read from it, or, as was often the case, portions were learned by heart and recited to eager listeners.

Rome arose in mighty wrath to crush the heresy of scripture reading in anything but Latin. Magistrates in every Christian country were directed to condemn to death all proven guilty of sustaining the doctrines of Wycliffe if they refused to abjure the same. In England all who taught without the license of the bishops were imprisoned and brought to trial within three months. If they were found guilty but willing to recant, they were fined and returned to prison; if they were previous offenders or refused to abjure, they were turned over to the civil authorities to be burned in a public place. This intense persecution, which led to many a martyr, brought the movement to a near halt; yet in 1519 we still read of seven people who were burned at Coventry for the crime of teaching their children and servants the Lord's prayer and the Ten Commandments in English, and of another person burned alive at Newbury for having read to a friend out of the English Bible.

The movement to get the Bible into the hands of the people was given new life in the sixteenth century by a young student of language named William Tyndale. Like Wycliffe, Tyndale was an Oxford scholar whose course became fixed in a debate with the clergy. In a particular argument the priests maintained, "We had better be without God's laws than the popes." To this the indignant Tyndale prophetically declared, "I defy the pope, and all his laws; and if God spare me I will one day make the boy that drives the plough in England to know more of scripture than the pope himself." (Foxe, p. 351.) Tyndale hid in London and commenced his life's labor; but, seeing men taken to prison and death for owning or reading the German translation of the Bible done by the rebel priest Martin Luther, he recognized the necessity of flight to Europe. There he translated the New Testament for the first time in English directly from the He-

brew and Greek manuscripts. Thanks to Johann Guten-
berg's discovery of movable type, thousands of copies
were printed and shipped to England. The Bible quite
literally became a hidden treasure; secreted in barrels
and boxes, in bolts of cloth, or in sacks of flour, many
copies were successfully smuggled past the watchful eye
of the clergy who guarded the ports. Once in the posses-
sion of the common people, the Bibles were quickly
spread through the length and breadth of the country.
Before he was able to complete his translation of the Old
Testament, Tyndale was betrayed; he was subsequently
imprisoned for nearly two years before he was con-
demned for heresy and sentenced to death. On October
6, 1536, he was bound to the stake and strangled, and his
dead body burned to ashes.

Seventy years after Tyndale's death, King James I directed that a new translation of the Bible be made. He appointed fifty-four scholars to the labor. Using the oldest
available manuscripts, they produced a masterpiece of
English literature at a time when the language was at its
richest and most creative in vocabulary, rhythm, and
style. To this day the King James or Authorized Version
remains unsurpassed in literary excellence. This was the
Bible of Joseph Smith, the Bible of the Restoration, the
Bible whose beautiful phraseology was picked up time
and again in the revelations of the Restoration. It thus
dictated the language and style in which the revelations
given to Joseph Smith would be clothed.

13. *To what extent can we trust Bible translations?*

Scholars are a confident lot, and perhaps none more
so than Bible translators, who without hesitation claim
that there could not possibly be more than one-tenth of
one percent chance of error in what they have translated.
Yet ever since Joseph Smith's statement that "we believe
the Bible to be the word of God as far as it is translated
correctly," Latter-day Saints have been skeptical and sus-
picious of translators, assuming that anything that does

not seem to harmonize with modern revelation is the result of faulty translation. Such is not the case, and even allowing for the vanity of the translators, they have translated accurately and responsibly. Admittedly, even in the best of circumstances theirs is a difficult task. It is no small matter for us today to take the Book of Mormon and correctly translate it into different languages; some errors will inevitably creep into the text in various languages. This has happened to the Bible, where the problem has been enhanced by theological ignorance, biases, and special interests of Bible translators.

Still, this is not the great issue, and it was not the great concern of the Prophet Joseph Smith. The more serious issue is that of the reliability of the manuscripts from which the translations have come. Both revelation and history testify that many corruptions exist in the ancient Bible texts. Thus Joseph Smith's testimony was "I believe the Bible as it read when it came from the pen of the original writers. Ignorant translators, careless transcribers, or designing and corrupt priests have committed many errors." (HC 6:57.)

The Lord told Moses that many of the words he (Moses) wrote would be taken from the book he would write. (Moses 1:41.) Through vision Nephi saw that a great and abominable church would take away from the "gospel of the Lamb many parts which are plain and most precious; and also many covenants of the Lord have they taken away." (1 Nephi 13:26.) Prefacing the vision on the degrees of glory, Joseph Smith declared: "From sundry revelations which have been received, it was apparent that many important points touching the salvation of man had been taken from the Bible, or lost before it was compiled." (D&C 76; HC 1:245.) Jeremiah wrote, "How can you say, 'We are wise, we have the law of the Lord,' when scribes with their lying pens have falsified it?" (Jeremiah 8:8, New English Translation.) John the Revelator, having seen so many of the scriptural texts

tampered with, sealed the book of Revelation with a
warning and a curse to any who dared tamper with what
he had written.

The New Testament books were copied thousands of
times, in many instances by untrained copyists, which resulted in an enormous number of errors. In fact, no two
of the five thousand existent New Testament manuscripts are exactly alike; obviously they cannot all be correct or true. As the number of manuscripts increases, the
number of scribal errors increases proportionately, yet it
is argued that this also increases proportionately the
means of correcting such errors. Again, for the most part
this has been accomplished in a magnificent manner by
responsible scholars. The scholars admit the difficulties
of language and the variants caused by human error.
The emphasis of latter-day revelation is with omissions
and in some instances interpolations at the hands of men
who deliberately altered the text with the intent to de-
ceive.

14. *What is the Joseph Smith translation of the Bible?*

By divine commission Joseph Smith made a revision
or translation of the King James Bible. He commenced
his work in June 1830 and completed the major portion
of it by July 1833. The work was constantly interrupted,
and he was still making modifications in the text, while
preparing it for publication, at the time of his death in
1844. It is assumed that he desired to make further
changes in it. The work contains many restorations of ancient texts that are still lost to the world and many other
helpful changes.

The eight chapters of the Book of Moses in the Pearl
of Great Price come from the Joseph Smith Translation
and illustrate the nature of the plain and precious truths
that have been taken from the Bible record. Though it
has never been adopted as the official Bible of The
Church of Jesus Christ of Latter-day Saints, the Joseph

Smith Translation is an invaluable study companion to every serious student of the gospel within the Church.

15. *Is the Bible the word of God?*

Of the Bible Brigham Young said, "I believe the words of God are there; I believe the words of the devil are there; I believe that the words of men and the words of angels are there; and that is not all—I believe that the words of a dumb brute are there. I recollect one of the prophets riding, and prophesying against Israel, and the animal he rode rebuked his madness." (JD 14:280.)

Notwithstanding all its difficulties, the Bible contains the word of God as it was given to his people through his prophets in ages past. Certainly one of its greatest messages is that whenever the God of heaven has had a people on the earth that he has recognized as his own, he has spoken to them through living prophets. The concepts and doctrines it contains are indeed his mind and will, though in most instances it has been left to the particular prophet to clothe them with language; thus the style of the various books differs greatly while the doctrine and the spirit are the same.

16. *What do our latter-day scriptures say about the Bible?*

The testimony of the ancient American prophet Mormon was that the Book of Mormon had been written for the very purpose of getting men to believe in the Bible. (Mormon 7:8-9.) In the revelation directing Joseph Smith to organize the Church, the Lord said that the Book of Mormon had come forth to prove to the world that the "holy scriptures were true," and that God had called prophets in this day to illustrate that he is the same, yesterday, today, and forever. (D&C 20:8-12.) In the revelation known as the Law of the Church, section 42 of the Doctrine and Covenants, the Lord directed that those who teach the gospel are to do so out of "the Bible and the Book of Mormon," in which, he declared, is found "the fulness of the gospel." (D&C 42:12.)

Just as the New Testament constantly testifies of the
validity of the Old Testament by drawing upon its teachings, quoting its prophets, and announcing itself to be
the fulfillment of many of its prophecies, so the Doctrine
and Covenants, Pearl of Great Price, and Book of Mormon constantly testify of the Bible and the great truths it
contains.

17. *Do the Latter-day Saints believe the Bible?*

The testimony of all Latter-day Saint prophets has
been and is that if the Book of Mormon is true, the Bible
is true. If one be true, they both are true; and if one be
false, they both are false. In response to the question "Do
the Mormons believe in the Bible," Joseph Smith said, "If
we do, we are the only people under heaven that does,
for there are none of the religious sects of the day that
do." Then in response to the question "Wherein do you
differ from other sects," the Prophet answered, "In that
we believe the Bible, and all other sects profess to believe
their interpretations of the Bible, and their creeds." (HC
3:28.) Brigham Young stated the matter in these words:
"It has been proclaimed that there is a great difference
between us and the Christian world. . . . The difference
arises from the fact that we believe this Bible, wide open,
from Genesis to Revelation. They believe it, sealed up,
never to be opened again to the human family. They
believe it shut, we believe it open; they believe it in silence, we believe it proclaimed on the house top." (JD
15:41.)

Chapter Eight

The Second Witness

Thou fool, that shall say: A Bible, we have got a Bible, and we need no more Bible. Have ye obtained a Bible save it were by the Jews?

Know ye not that there are more nations than one? Know ye not that I, the Lord your God, have created all men, and that I remember those who are upon the isles of the sea; and that I rule in the heavens above and in the earth beneath; and I bring forth my word unto the children of men, yea, even upon all the nations of the earth?

Wherefore murmur ye, because that ye shall receive more of my word? Know ye not that the testimony of two nations is a witness unto you that I am God, that I remember one nation like unto another? Wherefore, I speak the same words unto one nation like unto another. And when the two nations shall run together the testimony of the two nations shall run together also.

And I do this that they may prove unto many that I am the same yesterday, today, and forever; and that I speak forth my words according to mine own pleasure. And because that I have spoken one word ye need not suppose that I cannot speak another; for my work is not yet finished; neither shall it be until the end of man, neither from that time henceforth and forever.

Wherefore, because that ye have a Bible ye need not suppose that it contains all my words; neither need ye suppose that I have not caused more to be written. (2 Nephi 29:6-10.)

By the spirit of prophecy the Book of Mormon prophets knew that when the record containing their teachings and testimony came forth, many would reject it for no other reason than that they already had some fragments of the sermons and writings of ancient prophets in the old world. Strangely enough, there is nothing unusual in this, for the very chain that binds all the religions of men together is their common desire to seal the heavens and close the mouth of God while professing a love and reverence for his word. The Jews have their Torah, the Christians their Bible, the Islams the Koran, but none will admit more. All agree that the heavens are to be sealed, that God is to remain mute. At issue is only the time and place at which the veil of silence was dropped. Did the heavens exhaust their knowledge with Moses or Malachi, or with the apostles, or was Mohammed "the last of the prophets"? When the apostles went forth to teach at the time of Christ, the Jews rejected their message of additional revelation, declaring, "We have the law for our salvation, and that is sufficient for us." (JST Matthew 7:15.) Such it appears has been the litany of apostate religion from time immemorial.

In the revelation directing Joseph Smith to proceed with the organization of the Church, the Lord testified as to the truthfulness of the Book of Mormon and indicated that he had given it to the world as proof that "the holy scriptures are true, and that God does inspire men and call them to his holy work in this age and generation, as well as in generations of old; thereby showing that he is the same God yesterday, today, and forever." (D&C 20:11-12.) Three specific ideas are mentioned here: first, that the Book of Mormon constitutes our proof that the Bible is true; second, that the Book of Mormon is our witness or proof that Joseph Smith is the great prophet of the restoration; and third, that through the Book of Mormon we can once more know the God of heaven, a

God who changes not, a God who grants the same privilege of seeing and knowing and hearing eternal truths to men of all ages. Let us briefly examine each of these concepts along with other revealed statements in which the Lord declares his purposes in sending the Book of Mormon forth to the world.

The Book of Mormon as Proof That the Bible Is True

Since the Bible prophesies of the coming forth of the Book of Mormon, the very existence of the book proclaims the inspiration of the Bible. (See JST, Genesis 50:24-26; Ezekiel 37:15-19; 2 Nephi 3; Isaiah 29:9-24; 2 Nephi 27; D&C 27:5.) Further, the Book of Mormon stands as an independent testimony or witness of Bible events and doctrines. Book of Mormon prophets taught and testified of Adam and Eve; of Noah, Melchizedek, Abraham, Isaac, Jacob, Joseph, Isaiah, and Jeremiah; of the prophet who would prepare the way before the Savior; of Mary; of John (the Revelator); of the Twelve, and, of course, above all else of Christ. The faith and doctrines of the old world became the faith and doctrines of the new. They were members of the same church, held the same priesthood, administered the same ordinances, taught the same doctrines, and worshipped the same God, and did so in the name of the same Christ. The testimony of both Bible and Book of Mormon is of one fold and one shepherd. (Ezekiel 37:22-24; John 10:16; 3 Nephi 15:17-21.)

Directing his writings to the Lamanites in a day when they would receive the Book of Mormon, Mormon himself wrote: "Repent, and be baptized in the name of Jesus, and lay hold upon the gospel of Christ, which shall be set before you, not only in this record but also in the record which shall come unto the Gentiles from the Jews, which record shall come from the Gentiles unto you. For behold, this is written for the intent that ye may believe that; and if ye believe that ye will believe this also; and if ye believe this ye will know concerning your fathers, and also the marvelous works which were wrought by the power of God among them." (Mormon 7:8-9.)

The Book of Mormon as Proof That Joseph Smith Is a Prophet

The Book of Mormon contains the promise that those who prayerfully study it will know that it is of God. The simple test given by the missionaries to sincere investigators is that in reading the book they stop twice on each page and ask, "Could Joseph Smith have written this?" When the volume is completed, the question will have been asked and answered over a thousand times. The Spirit will have left its indelible imprint on the heart of the reader, who will now know with a surety that Joseph Smith is a prophet.

When members of the Church met in conference to gather a collection of the revelations of the Prophet Joseph Smith for publication in what was then to be known as the Book of Commandments, some concern and embarrassment were expressed about the language of the revelations. The Lord responded to those entertaining such doubts with the invitation for them to produce a revelation like unto the very least of those penned by the Prophet. William E. McLellin, who the Prophet noted had "more learning than sense," attempted to do just that. McLellin failed miserably while demonstrating that "it was an awful responsibility to write in the name of the Lord." (HC 1:226.) How much greater, then, to take up the challenge of producing a book with the depth and breadth of the Book of Mormon! The Book of Mormon is a tangible evidence that the gift and power of God rested upon the Prophet Joseph Smith.

The Book of Mormon as Proof of an Unchanging God

Having learned of the great things revealed to Lehi, his father, Nephi was desirous to "see, and hear, and

know" those same things and to do so by the "power of
the Holy Ghost," which he described as "the gift of God
unto all those who diligently seek him, as well in times of
old as in the time that he should manifest himself unto
the children of men." For Nephi declared, "He is the
same yesterday, to-day, and forever; and the way is prepared for all men from the foundation of the world, if it
so be that they repent and come unto him. For he that
diligently seeketh shall find; and the mysteries of God
shall be unfolded unto them, by the power of the Holy
Ghost, as well in these times as in times of old, and as well
in times of old as in times to come; wherefore, the course
of the Lord is one eternal round." (1 Nephi 10:17-19.)

Long before the birth of Christ, the prophet Alma
asked: "Is not a soul at this time as precious unto God as a
soul will be at the time of his coming? Is it not as necessary
that the plan of redemption should be made known unto
this people as well as unto their children? Is it not as easy
at this time for the Lord to send his angel to declare these
glad tidings unto us as unto our children, or as after the
time of his coming?" (Alma 39:17-19.)

To such questions we respond with a resounding
"Yes!" for the Book of Mormon has restored to us a
knowledge of the God of our fathers, a God who will
speak to us and call from among our midst prophets as
he did in times past, a God who is the same yesterday,
today, and forever.

The Book of Mormon Confounds False Doctrines

The most damning heresies are those that stand in
opposition to the most basic of saving truths. Such doctrines deny the reality and nature of God; they rob him
of the glory of creation and seek to reduce him to a body-
less, partless, passionless being. Of him they say that he
once wandered the earth as a miracle-performing ethics
teacher, one who now, having done his work, has retired
to yonder heavens where he sits enthroned in mute si-

lence. To such, the fall of Adam is but figure and myth and the Atonement unnecessary and primitive. The list goes on and on, for such errors become the parents of a thousand more. Gospel ordinances are said to be but outward signs and thus unnecessary, while spiritual gifts, angels, dreams, revelations, and miracles are all said to be things of the past. They profess God yet deny his power; they declare love for his word yet refuse to hear his voice; they exalt the ancient prophets yet reject those who come in the name of the Master; they marvel at his miracles yet deny all such to those of our day.

To all such, as a voice from the dust, thunders the testimony of the prophets of the Book of Mormon:

> I speak unto you who deny the revelations of God, and say that they are done away, that there are no revelations, nor prophecies, nor gifts, nor healing, nor speaking with tongues, and the interpretation of tongues;
>
> Behold I say unto you, he that denieth these things knoweth not the gospel of Christ; yea, he has not read the scriptures; if so, he does not understand them.
>
> For do we not read that God is the same yesterday, today, and forever, and in him there is no variableness neither shadow of changing?
>
> And now, if ye have imagined up unto yourselves a god who doth vary, and in whom there is shadow of changing, then have ye imagined up unto yourselves a god who is not a God of miracles.
>
> But behold, I will show unto you a God of miracles, even the God of Abraham, and the God of Isaac, and the God of Jacob; and it is that same God who created the heavens and the earth, and all things that in them are.
>
> Behold, he created Adam, and by Adam came the fall of man. And because of the fall of man came Jesus Christ, even the Father and the Son; and because of Jesus Christ came the redemption of man.
>
> And because of the redemption of man, which came by Jesus Christ, they are brought back into the presence of the Lord; yea, this is wherein all men are redeemed, because the death of Christ bringeth to pass the resurrection. . . .

And then cometh the judgment of the Holy One upon them. . . .

O all ye that have imagined up unto yourselves a god who can do no miracles, I would ask of you, have all these things passed, of which I have spoken? Has the end come yet? Behold I say unto you, Nay; and God has not ceased to be a God of miracles. . . .

And behold, I say unto you he changeth not; if so he would cease to be God; and he ceaseth not to be God, and is a God of miracles.

And the reason why he ceaseth to do miracles among the children of men is because that they dwindle in unbelief, and depart from the right way, and know not the God in whom they should trust.

Behold, I say unto you that whoso believeth in Christ, doubting nothing, whatsoever he shall ask the Father in the name of Christ it shall be granted him; and this promise is unto all, even unto the ends of the earth. (Mormon 9:7-21.)

Through the sacred pages of the Bible we learn of the trials and faith of our ancient fathers, while through the pages of the Book of Mormon we are instructed by them. The Bible records God's words to the ancients; the Book of Mormon records the words of the ancients to us. It is to this volume that we turn to be taught in plainness and simplicity. It is in the Book of Mormon that we find the great discourses on faith, baptism, being spiritually born of God, the Holy Ghost, and the necessity of enduring to the end. It is the Book of Mormon that most clearly teaches the divine sonship of Christ, defines the gospel, divides the spirit world into paradise and hell, and provides descriptions of those who will inherit both. It is the Book of Mormon that defines the Resurrection, prophetically describes the churches of the last days, gives a description of the New Jerusalem that is to be built in the Americas, and describes the return of scattered Israel to Christ and the Church and thence to the lands of their inheritance. For teaching the doctrines of the gospel, the Book of Mormon, even among sacred writ, is without peer.

The Two Records Sustain Each Other

Describing the relationship that was to exist between the Book of Mormon (stick of Joseph) and the Bible (stick of Judah), Ezekiel said they were to become as "one stick" or book in the hands of the two houses of Israel. (Ezekiel 37:17.) In like manner, Joseph of Egypt said they would "grow together." (2 Nephi 3:12.) In our dispensation, even before the translation of the Book of Mormon had been completed, the Lord assured Joseph Smith that he had not brought it forth to "destroy" the Bible but rather to "build it up." (D&C 10:52.) The union of the two books can be likened to a good marriage. Having become as one in the household of faith, they begin to grow closer and closer together as the years pass and as our understanding of them increases.

There is a strength in the union of the two books that neither has alone. Most often it is to the Bible that we turn to find out *what* happened anciently and then to the Book of Mormon to find out *why* it happened. For instance, the Bible gives us an account of the fall of Adam, while it is to the Book of Mormon that we must turn to find out why the fall was necessary. "If Adam had not transgressed," Lehi explained, "he would not have fallen, but he would have remained in the garden of Eden. And all things which were created must have remained in the same state in which they were after they were created; and they must have remained forever, and had no end. And they would have had no children; wherefore they would have remained in a state of innocence, having no joy, for they knew no misery; doing no good, for they knew no sin. But behold, all things have been done in the wisdom of him who knoweth all things. Adam fell that men might be; and men are, that they might have joy." (2 Nephi 2:22-25.)

In like manner the New Testament writers tell us the dramatic story of the passion week. From them we learn, virtually hour by hour, the events of that last day that led to Gethsemane and then the cross. It is a moving account from which all who read it grow in love and appreciation to the Savior for what he suffered for each of us. Yet once again it is to the prophets of the Book of Mormon that we turn to learn why such a sacrifice was necessary. (See Alma 34:13-16; 40.)

Emphasizing the absolute necessity of the Atonement, Nephi's brother Jacob explained what would have become of all the children of men had no atonement been made. The spirits of all men, he taught, would have been trapped in the spirit prison for an endless duration. Not only would there have been no resurrection, but our spirits would have been subject to the devil to become "like unto him . . . devils, angels to a devil, to be shut out from the presnce of our God, and to remain with the father of lies, in misery" forever and ever. (2 Nephi 9: 7-9.)

The Bible tells us how the law of Moses was given, and the Book of Mormon explains why it was given. (Mosiah 13:27-35.) The Gospel writers tell us the story of Christ's baptism, but it is left to Nephi to explain why it was necessary that the sinless one be baptized. (2 Nephi 31:5-10.)

Consistently we find the Bible preserving the story and the Book of Mormon explaining its true importance. Thus it is in the union of these two books that we see the fulfillment of the prophecy of Joseph of Egypt that the stick of Joseph and the stick of Judah would "grow together unto the confounding of false doctrines and laying down of contentions, and establishing peace" among his descendants and also bring them to the knowledge of their fathers as well as the special promises that the Lord has made with Israel. (JST, Genesis 50:31; 2 Nephi 3:12.)

Getting Nearer to God

It is difficult to overstate the importance of the Book of Mormon, especially as we give consideration to the operations of the spirit of revelation. Joseph Smith said that "the Book of Mormon was the most correct of any book on earth, and the keystone of our religion, and a man would get nearer to God by abiding by its precepts, than by any other book." (HC 4:461.) Those sincerely desiring to draw nearer to God and his spirit have greater opportunity to do so in the pages of this book than those of any other.

Chapter Nine

Revelations of the Restoration

Take away the Book of Mormon and the revelations, and where is our religion? We have none. (Joseph Smith, HC 2:52.)

Though we describe both the Bible and the Book of Mormon with superlatives—especially as they are used together—they are not in and of themselves sufficient for our generation. To so regard either book or the combination of the two would be to deny their spirit, testimony, and purpose.

Teaching this principle, John Taylor observed that "Adam's revelation did not instruct Noah to build his ark; nor did Noah's revelation tell Lot to forsake Sodom; nor did either of these speak of the departure of the children of Israel from Egypt. These all had revelations for themselves, and so had Isaiah, Jeremiah, Ezekiel, Jesus, Peter, Paul, John, Joseph, and so must we, or we shall make a shipwreck." (*Millennial Star,* November 1, 1847, p. 323.) Just as the lame man at the temple gate was commanded by Peter to rise and walk, so that same priesthood requires of all men in all ages that they stand on their own feet and work out their own salvation with fear and trembling. All must have their own revelation, prophets, and scriptures, as they must have their own faith, repentance and baptism.

The Voice of Warning

Indeed, the issue is not whether God speaks but rather who is willing to listen! "Wherefore," we are told in the revealed preface to the Doctrine and Covenants, "the voice of the Lord is unto the ends of the earth, that all that will hear may hear." (D&C 1:11.) This revelation, which has been designated "the voice of warning," introduces Joseph Smith and the message of the restoration to the world. It invites all to come and listen to a prophet's voice, for the Lord, knowing the calamity that is to come upon a wicked world, announces that he has called Joseph Smith, spoken to him from the heavens, given him commandments, and commissioned him to proclaim these things to the world. The Lord declared that all of this came in fulfillment of that which the ancient prophets had written in his name. Sealing his testimony, he declares: "What I the Lord have spoken, I have spoken, and I excuse not myself; and though the heavens and the earth pass away, my word shall not pass away, but shall all be fulfilled, whether by mine own voice or by the voice of my servants, it is the same." (D&C 1:38.)

The heart of this revelation is that the arm of the Lord has been revealed and the day soon cometh when "they who will not hear the voice of the Lord, neither the voice of his servants, neither give heed to the words of the prophets and apostles, shall be cut off from among the people." (D&C 1:14.) Again the prophecy is but the echo of the testimony of prophets and righteous men from the earliest of times, all of whom anticipated those days and events which we now approach. (Deuteronomy 18:15-19; Acts 3:22; 1 Nephi 22:21; 3 Nephi 20:23; JS–H 1:40.)

A Key to the Past

We live in what the scriptures describe as the dispensation of the fulness of times, meaning that era of the earth's history in which all gospel knowledge and authority of dispensations past is to be restored. We make no profession to a new gospel but rather to the bringing back of the same truths and authority by which men were saved anciently. The distinctive claim of Mormonism is in its antiquity, not its newness. Joseph Smith professed the gospel of Peter, James, John, and Paul, testifying that all were one and the same as that professed by the Lord Jesus Christ himself. The world has chosen to call this Mormonism, but they could as well have chosen to call it Adamism, Enochism, Noahism, Abrahamism, or named it after any faithful prophet of any age, for all held to the same truths and were loyal to the same God. They were members of the same church, held the same priesthood, and participated in the same ordinances of salvation.

The Prophet described our dispensation as the "complete and perfect union," the "welding together" of all the rights, keys, honors, majesty, glory, power, and priesthood of past dispensations. Thus the story of the Restoration as it unfolds in the compilation of revelations found in the Doctrine and Covenants constitutes a great Urim and Thummim through which we can view and understand events and doctrines in the Old and New Testaments. It is for us both map and compass to the rich treasures of the past. It gives perspective, direction, meaning, and understanding to our study of the Bible that is in many instances light years ahead of that which we can gain from sectarian commentaries, archaeological digs, and such finds as the Dead Sea Scrolls and the Ebla Tablets.

A Revealed Commentary

To attempt to study the Bible without the aid of the Doctrine and Covenants and other revelations of the restoration would be a serious mistake in gospel scholarship. Surely no one with a testimony of the Restoration would turn to sectarian commentaries for an explanation of the parable of the wheat and the tares when in the

Doctrine and Covenants the Lord gives his own explanation of what he meant. (D&C 86.) In like manner the
world may debate the Savior's meaning when he said that
he and the Father would make their abode with those
who loved them and kept the commandments, but for
the Latter-day Saints there is no cause for misunderstanding. In the Doctrine and Covenants we read:
"John 14:23—The appearing of the Father and the Son,
in that verse, is a personal appearance; and the idea that
the Father and the Son dwell in a man's heart is an old
sectarian notion, and is false." (D&C 130:3.) Again, one
would not want to read the prophecy of Daniel about the
return of the Ancient of Days without reading section
116, which identifies the Ancient of Days as Adam and
the place of his return as the ancient city of Adam-ondi-
Ahman, or what is known to us as Spring Hill, Daviess
County, Missouri.

As a people we respect scholarship, yet the works of
the world's greatest scholars are as nothing when compared with the revelations of heaven. As Joseph Smith
said, "Could you gaze into heaven five minutes, you
would know more than you would by reading all that
ever was written on the subject." (HC 6:50.)

In some instances the Doctrine and Covenants will
comment on a specific Bible passage, citing the verse in
question. In most instances, however, the revelations in
the Doctrine and Covenants will just pick up the language of the Bible and amplify its meaning, announce its
fulfillment, or place it in a context that sheds considerable light on its Bible usage. For instance, section 133, a
revelation on the last days and the coming of Christ,
weaves together scores of prophecies from the Old and
New Testaments. It sheds light on them all and gives
specific commentary on some. As a specific illustration, it
picks up the language of John the Revelator when he
described an angel he saw flying in the midst of heaven
with the everlasting gospel, which was to be committed

again to men upon the earth. (Revelation 14:6-7.) In the complete sense the prophecy embraces all the ancient prophets who were to return to restore authority and keys, though in this instance the prophecy is given in the past tense (D&C 133:36), emphasizing the role of Moroni and the coming forth of the Book of Mormon in which is found that gospel which must be preached among every nation, kindred, tongue, and people.

To further illustrate the role of the Doctrine and Covenants as a revealed or divine commentary, the reader is invited to consider the following sections:

Section 74 is an explanation of counsel given by the apostle Paul to the Corinthian saints in 1 Corinthians 7.

Section 77 contains a series of questions and revealed answers on the Book of Revelation.

Section 113 contains a series of questions and revealed answers on the prophecies of Isaiah.

Section 132 explains the doctrine of marriage as taught by the Savior, picking up the language of Matthew 22:30; it also gives revealed insights into the doctrine of plurality of wives as practiced by Abraham, Isaac, and Jacob.

Restoring the Knowledge of the Ancients

In addition to providing inspired commentary on Bible passages, the Doctrine and Covenants is the source of much information about the ancient saints and their knowledge of the gospel plan, knowledge that has long since been lost to the world. A few brief illustrations are as follows:

Section 45 is an expansion of the Savior's discourse on the signs of the times as given on the Mount of Olives. (Matthew 24.)

Section 63:21 extends our knowledge of the experience Peter, James, and John shared with the Savior on the mount of transfiguration. They saw the renewal of the earth and its return to a paradisiacal state.

Section 76 extends the Savior's statement that in his Father's house are many mansions (John 14:2), and John's statement about a resurrection of the just and the unjust. This is the great revelation on the degrees of glory.

Section 88 picks up the language of the apostle Paul's discourse on the resurrection (1 Corinthians 15), explaining the nature of the bodies men will have in the worlds to come.

Section 93 includes an excerpt from the Gospel of John the Baptist now lost to us, with the promise that it will yet be restored.

Section 138 expands the reference of Peter about the visit of Christ to the spirits in prison during the period that His body lay in the tomb. (1 Peter 3:18-20.) This is a great revelation on the manner in which the gospel is taught in the world of the spirits.

Announcing and Foreshadowing the Fulfillment of Bible Prophecy

The Doctrine and Covenants is both an announcement to the world of the fulfillment of some of the ancient prophecies and a new witness that others of those prophecies are about to be fulfilled. Consider the following as illustrations:

Daniel 2 recounts the story of Nebuchadnezzar's dream and Daniel's interpretation of it. The king saw a great image, a stone cut from the mountain without hands that destroyed the image and then rolled forth to fill the whole earth. Section 65 announces the manner of fulfillment of this prophecy.

Malachi 3 foretells the coming of a messenger to prepare the way for the coming of Christ. If the message is the gospel as the Doctrine and Covenants declares, then Joseph Smith is the messenger. (D&C 45:9.) The prophecy also foreshadows the return of John the Baptist and the restoration of that priesthood which will enable the sons of Levi to "offer unto the Lord an offering in righteousness." That authority was restored by John the Baptist to Joseph Smith on May 15, 1829.

Malachi 4 is the prophecy of the coming of Elijah before the great and dreadful day of the Lord's return. Section 2 contains Moroni's paraphrase of this prophecy as rendered to Joseph Smith in 1823. Doctrine and Covenants 110:13-16 contains the scriptural account of Elijah's return, while Doctrine and Covenants 128:17-18 explains the implications of the authority restored by Elijah.

A Guide for the Last Days

The Doctrine and Covenants is a survival manual for the last days. Not only does it warn us of the "evils and designs which do and will exist in the hearts of conspiring men" (D&C 89:4), but it also teaches us principles of discernment in order that we will not "be seduced by evil spirits, or doctrines of devils, or the commandments of men; for some are of men, and others of devils" (D&C 46:7). "Men are ignorant of the nature of spirits," Joseph Smith said; they know nothing of "their power, laws, government, intelligence, etc." (HC 4:572.) It is to the revelations of the Doctrine and Covenants that we turn to find "a pattern in all things," that we "may not be deceived." (D&C 52:14.)

Further, it is to this compilation of revelations that we turn to learn the signs of the times, for to the Saints it is given "to know the signs of the times, and the signs of the coming of the Son of Man." (D&C 68:11.) To the world his coming is to be as the "thief in the night," but to the "children of light" his coming is to be as "travail upon a woman with child." (D&C 106:4-5; 1 Thessalonians 5:2-3.) Repeatedly the warning has been given that we are to stand in holy places (D&C 45:32; 87:8; 101:22, 64), which places of refuge have been identified as the "land of Zion" and "her stakes" (D&C 115:6), while those of

Judah are to flee to Jerusalem (D&C 124:36; 133:12-13).
There is but one place of safety for the Latter-day Saints,
and that is to be found standing in mind, spirit, and deed
at the side of their prophets. On the day of the organization of the Church, the Lord described the relationship
between the Saints and the Prophet, saying: "Thou shalt
give heed unto all his words and commandments which
he shall give unto you as he receiveth them, walking in all
holiness before me; for his word ye shall receive, as if
from mine own mouth, in all patience and faith. For by
doing these things the gates of hell shall not prevail
against you; yea, the Lord God will disperse the powers
of darkness from before you, and cause the heavens
to shake for your good, and his name's glory." (D&C 21:
4-6.)

Church Doctrine and Government

Within the covers of the Doctrine and Covenants,
"the doctrines of the gospel are set forth with explana-
tions about such fundamental matters as the nature of
the Godhead, the origin of man, the reality of Satan, the
purpose of mortality, the necessity for obedience, the
need for repentance, the workings of the Holy Spirit, the
ordinances and performances that pertain to salvation,
the destiny of the earth, the future conditions of man
after the resurrection and the judgment, the eternity of
the marriage relationship, and the eternal nature of the
family. Likewise the gradual unfolding of the adminis-
trative structure of the Church is shown with the calling
of bishops, the First Presidency, the Council of the
Twelve, and the Seventy, and the establishment of other
presiding offices and quorums. Finally, the testimony
that is given of Jesus Christ—his divinity, his majesty, his
perfection, his love, and his redeeming power—makes
this book of great value to the human family and of more
worth than the riches of the whole earth." (Explanatory
Introduction to the Doctrine and Covenants.)

The Duty of the Saints

In the Doctrine and Covenants the Saints are instructed in those matters essential to their own salvation. They are told of the obligation that rests upon them as a Church to gather the elect from the ends of the earth and to do the work of redeeming their dead in the temples of the Lord so that the gospel may indeed go to all peoples.

We Stand Independent

Just as children receive their very lifeblood from their parents, so we as a church have received from our fathers of dispensations past every key, power, grace, and authority that we possess. Yet as children are, at the proper time, to leave father and mother and stand independent, so we as a church stand independent of all past dispensations. They gave us life, and we are welded to them by love and those authorities we inherited from them. They have taught us much, and yet we can, and indeed do, stand independent of them. It is for us to continue the journey they started, not just retread the paths they trod. We are not dependent on the revelations of past dispensations to find the path leading to the kingdom of God. Our guides are living oracles, our dispensation has its own revelations, and all saving truths and ordinances have been revealed anew. The power is in us to save ourselves. The constitution of the Church in all dispensations is living prophets, not ancient records. Where the churches of the world have attempted to rebuild on the rubble of the past, we have taken the divine blueprint and built anew. The doctrines of the ancient saints are our doctrines; their faith is now our faith. Just as they had living prophets and added to the canon of scripture, so do we. Through their prophets and revelations they knew of our day, and through our prophets and revelations we know of theirs.

Chapter Ten

The Pearl of Great Price

Again, the kingdom of heaven is like unto a merchant man, seeking goodly pearls: Who, when he had found one pearl of great price, went and sold all that he had, and bought it. (Matthew 13:45-46.)

The Pearl of Great Price is the briefest and yet most expansive of our scriptural records. It was left to this marvelous little compilation of revelations to bind the eternities together. Let us liken it as we did the Doctrine and Covenants to a seerstone or the Urim and Thummim, for through it we also view both past and future. It is in this volume that we learn of the grand council of heaven, the council where the Gods laid the plans whereby the earth was created; that we read an Inspired Version account of the creation of the earth, and that we receive an expanded account of the fall of Adam. Here it is that we read of the generations of Adam, Enoch, Noah, Abraham, Moses, Christ, and Joseph Smith. Each of the major gospel dispensations is briefly viewed, all of them from the perspective of a plan ordained even before the act of creation. From this volume we learn that Enoch was told "all the doings of the children of men," and that Abraham saw those whom the Lord had appointed to be his rulers from among the host of pre-earth spirits. Thus the volume becomes to us as Moses' experience on the high mountain was to him. As Moses was enabled to see "the world and the ends thereof, and all the children of men," so through the pages of this inspired volume we may see and know of the same things.

This volume is a unique expression of the prophetic powers of Joseph Smith. In it he restores a portion of the writings of Adam, Enoch, Abraham, and Moses. The fragment restored from the writings of each of these ancient patriarchs not only reached beyond the knowledge of Joseph Smith's day, it also stretched beyond the richest of imaginations. Knowing that these books, which had been given to the Saints as a reward for their faith, would become a stone of stumbling and a rock of offense to the world, the Saints at that time were instructed to "show them not unto any except them that believe." (Moses 1:42; 5:32.) Notwithstanding the assaults of many a supposed scholar, these restored texts stand impregnable, a mountain peak affording a breathtaking view of both the past and the future.

Not only do these books testify of a God who changes not and of gospel principles that vary not so much as a jot or tittle from one dispensation to another, they are also a remarkable illustration of the plain and precious truths that have been taken from the Bible record. Here we read of the baptism of Adam, of the "grand Key-words of the Holy Priesthood" that were "revealed to Adam in the Garden of Eden, as also to Seth, Noah, Melchizedek, Abraham, and all to whom the Priesthood was revealed." (Book of Abraham, facsimile 2, figure 3.) From these texts we learn that the gospel taught by Noah and rejected by those destroyed in the flood was the gospel of repentance and of baptism in the name of Jesus Christ, with the attendant promise that those thus baptized would receive the Holy Ghost. It is in these revelations of the past that we find the clear depiction of the future.

The Pearl of Great Price consists of the Book of Moses, the Book of Abraham, Joseph Smith–Matthew,

Joseph Smith– History, and the Articles of Faith. Let us
briefly describe each.

The Book of Moses, or, as it is more correctly known,
"Selections from the Book of Moses," consists of eight
chapters, all of which come from the Joseph Smith
Translation of the Bible. The first chapter has been published as a preface to that work, though it has been left
out of the most recent edition. It is an account of some
experiences of Moses between the time the Lord spoke to
him from the burning bush and the exodus. In this chapter we learn that Moses was caught away in the spirit unto
an exceedingly high mountain where he talked with God
face to face. We learn of the necessity of his being trans-
figured in order to withstand the glory of God and then
how Moses detected Satan, when he came declaring himself to be the Only Begotten, because Satan was without
glory. After commanding the impostor to depart, Moses
was again enveloped in the power of God, which enabled
him to see the history of the earth, how it was created,
even "every particle of it," along with all of its inhabitants
both past and future. Moses also saw many other earths
but was given only an account of this earth and its inhabitants.

This experience was preparatory to Moses' writing of
the creative account that is found in the first two chapters
of Genesis or in its more correct translation, chapters two
and three of Moses. The other four chapters of the Book
of Moses extend the Inspired Version account of Genesis
down to near the time of the flood. The book is of great
significance to the inquirer after truth. From it we are assured (contrary to many scholarly arguments) that Moses
was the author of Genesis and that there never was a man
more capable or able to write the story of the Creation
than he, for with the power of God resting on him, he saw
the history of mother earth from the time of her creation
to the time of her redemption.

Many legends and traditions come from the Jews

about Moses' great powers of seership. In the *Legends of the Jews*, Ginzberg writes; "God revealed to him not only the complete history of Israel that was to take place in the Holy Land, but also revealed to him all that had occurred and that was to occur in the world, from its creation to the Day of Judgment, when the resurrection of the dead will take place." (*Legends* 3:443.) "He let him look into the future, and let him see every generation and its sages, every generation and its prophets, every generation and its expounders of the Scriptures, every generation and its leaders, every generation and its pious men." (*Legends* 3:136.)

As an interpolation in his account of the creation, Moses announces that all things were created spiritually first. (Moses 3:5.) Thus we are assured that all living things had an existence prior to earth life. The fourth chapter begins with a flashback to the preexistence, recounting part of the story of the grand council, when the Father, having taught the plan of salvation and explained the need for a Redeemer, asked, "Whom shall I send?" Both the Beloved Son and Lucifer responded. Christ sought the will of the Father while Satan sought only the honor and power of God. When the Father chose the Beloved Son to come to earth as our Redeemer, Lucifer rebelled and was cast out.

At this point Moses returns to his narrative, and we again join Adam and Eve in the Garden of Eden. Moses then tells the story of their transgression and expulsion from the Garden. In the fifth chapter we are told of the rebellion of Cain and how the family of Adam were taught the gospel by holy angels. The sixth chapter tells of the pure and undefiled language spoken at the time of Adam and how he and Eve taught their children to read and write; it also tells of the book of remembrance that was kept by his righteous posterity. In this chapter we are introduced to Enoch, the visionary giant, who was called "a wild man" and "a strange thing" by those to whom he preached. His peerless teachings on the fall, the redemption, and the need for baptism follow.

In the seventh chapter we are awed as Enoch commands mountains to flee, rivers to turn out of their course, and a land to be brought up out of the depth of the sea as a refuge or hiding place for his enemies. Here we read of the great City of Enoch, which was taken into heaven, and of Enoch's vision to the end of time, which includes the coming forth of the Book of Mormon, the gathering of Israel, and the building of the New Jerusalem.

In the eighth and final chapter we learn of Noah and how he and his sons taught to those of their generation the gospel of faith in Jesus Christ, repentance, and baptism. Their rejection and the wickedness of the people brought on the flood and destruction of a wicked world—a world that Enoch had been told was more wicked than any of the countless worlds that the Lord had created.

The Book of Abraham, which consists of five chapters and three facsimiles or drawings by Abraham, follows the Book of Moses. While the Book of Moses came by revelation and inspired correction of the Old Testament text, the book of Abraham is the result of a translation of some papyrus scrolls found in the catacombs of Egypt. In chapter one, Abraham tells how he sought the patriarchal order, of the idolatrous worship in the land of Chaldea where he lived, and how he was rescued from a sacrificial altar by an angel of the Lord. In the second chapter we find the purest account in the scriptures of the Abrahamic covenant. Abraham was promised that his seed would be rightful heirs to the priesthood and would be charged with the responsibility to take the message of salvation to all the families of the earth. In the third chapter we learn of a great revelation Abraham received through the Urim and Thummim about the sun, moon, and stars and the order of the heavens. Abraham was then taught that the order of these heavenly bodies typified the order of the heavenly kingdom or the government of God and the relation of the pre-earth spirits one to another. Abraham saw these pre-earth spirits and was shown how some had been designated by the Lord as "noble and great" and had been foreordained to be his rulers; he was also told that he was one of those so designated. Chapters four and five recount the plan of the Gods as they sat in council together and designated the order of the creation.

The first facsimile depicts Abraham's experience as he almost became a human sacrifice to the false gods of the Chaldeans. The second facsimile deals with Abraham's vision of the stars and the heavenly order of things, and contains references to the temple ritual and some things not yet revealed to our dispensation. The third facsimile represents Abraham's experience in Egypt, where he taught principles of astronomy in Pharaoh's court.

Joseph Smith–Matthew is the 24th chapter of Matthew as it was revealed to Joseph Smith in his work on the Inspired Translation. It is an appreciable improvement over the text of the King James and other translations. As no serious student of the Bible would study the Book of Genesis without the help of the Books of Moses and Abraham, so no student of the New Testament or of the last days would approach those subjects without the helps, clarifications, and restorations of this text.

Joseph Smith–History comes from the first five chapters of the *History of the Church*. It is the Joseph Smith story as it appears in the missionary tracts. Owing to the many evil and lying reports that had been written against the Church, Joseph Smith found it necessary to tell his own story. As no honest man would judge Christ by Gospels written by Caiaphas, Pilate, Herod, or Judas, so no honest man would judge Joseph Smith or the message of the Restoration by those things said and written by enemies of the Church. Joseph Smith is entitled to his day in court. All honest and fair-minded men who seek truth will take the opportunity to read his story as he told it.

The Articles of Faith are a brief statement of some of the fundamental truths associated with the restoration of the gospel. They are profitable for instruction but are not to be viewed as a creed.

Chapter Eleven

Manifestations of the Spirit

And we, ourselves, also, through the infinite goodness of God, and the manifestations of his Spirit, have great views of that which is to come; and were it expedient, we could prophesy of all things. (Mosiah 5:3.)

The promise of the Lord is that "whosoever believeth on my words, them will I visit with the manifestation of my Spirit." (D&C 5:16.) When Moses sought to stand in the presence of the Lord, he climbed the holy mount where he knew that presence to be. Through the scriptures we are invited to ascend our own Sinai, that we too might stand in that presence. If our desire is to stand on such holy ground, we would do well, like Moses, to ascend to those places from which we know the Lord has spoken. If we seek the Spirit, we must do so in the environment of the Spirit—and what better place to seek that voice than the majestic peaks of holy writ?

There is a special power and spirit associated with the word of the Lord, and it is found in the scriptures. Even as Nephi lamented over his inability to write, he acknowledged that the power of the Spirit would give that which he had written a special strength. (2 Nephi 33:4.) We rejoice in the contributions of the world's fine poets, writers, and philosophers. They have enriched life, but they cannot grant life; they can inspire, but they cannot exalt.

They cannot heal the sick, raise the dead, or create a celestial kingdom, nor can they preserve the family unit throughout the eternities. There is a power in faith that surpasses all that man can do. "Faith comes," declared Joseph Smith, "by hearing the word of God through the testimony of the servants of God—that testimony is always attended by the spirit of prophecy and revelation." (*The Words of Joseph Smith,* ed. Andrew F. Ehat and Lyndon W. Cook, Bookcraft, 1980, p. 3.) The Holy Ghost is a revelator; and where the word of God is found, the influence of the Holy Ghost will be found also.

There is no better place to learn to hear the whisperings of the spirit of revelation than in the scriptures. In a revelation directed to the Quorum of the Twelve (given some six years before they were called), the Lord said, "These words are not of men nor of man, but of me; wherefore, you shall testify they are of me and not of man; for it is my voice which speaketh them unto you; for they are given by my Spirit unto you, and by my power you can read them one to another; and save it were by my power you could not have them; wherefore, you can testify that you have heard my voice, and know my words." (D&C 18:34-36.) The promise is that these men at some future time, or for that matter at any future time, could take these revealed words and read them one to another under the influence and direction of the Spirit, and by so doing they would be entitled to testify that they had heard his voice. In principle, the promise is not limited to a specific group of men nor a particular revelation; rather, it extends to all who will read by the Spirit the word of the Lord. All who have done so have heard the voice of the Lord and are entitled to so testify.

Indolence and ignorance are not attractive to the Spirit. The Lord expects us to use our heads and do our homework. To Hyrum Smith, one of the best men who ever lived, the Lord said, "Seek not to declare my word, but first seek to obtain my word, and then shall your tongue be loosed; then, if you desire, you shall have my Spirit and my word, yea, the power of God unto the convincing of men. But now hold your peace; study my word which hath gone forth among the children of men, and also study my word which shall come forth among the children of men, or that which is now translating, yea, until you have obtained all which I shall grant unto the children of men in this generation, and then shall all things be added thereto." (D&C 11:21-22.) We cannot expect to effectively serve the Lord nor do we have any claim on the blessings of the Spirit until we have sought through meaningful study to know and understand his word. We can hardly profess to love the Lord while showing no interest in the revelations he has given us.

On the walls of Saint Peter's Basilica in Rome are artists' depictions of New Testament events. What is not immediately evident to the eye is that these marvelous treasures of art are not the work of an artist's brush, but are rather mosaics. These masterpieces were made by piecing together tens of thousands of bits of colored stone. In like manner are the prophetic descriptions of the scriptures, their hidden treasures, to be pieced together. It was never intended that such marvelous treasures be witnessed by those making only a nominal effort to find and see them. The prophecies of the scriptures constitute a great spiritual mosaic, one that can be pieced together and witnessed only by those who have both searched and pondered.

Opposition in All Things

Light and darkness will never meet. Christ and Satan will never shake hands. Joseph Smith taught us that "the nearer a person approaches the Lord, a greater power will be manifested by the adversary to prevent the accomplishment of His purposes." (Orson F. Whitney, *Life of Heber C. Kimball*, Stevens and Wallis, Inc., 1945, p. 132.) Such was his experience as he approached the Lord in what we know as the First Vision. As he knelt in prayer, he was seized upon by a power that entirely overcame him. Engulfed in thick darkness, his tongue bound, he thought himself doomed to destruction—"not to an imaginary ruin, but to the power of some actual being from the unseen world." (JS–H 1:15-16.) Later, Moroni was to promise him that his name would be known for "good and evil among all nations, kindreds, and tongues, or that it should be both good and evil spoken of among all people." (JS–H 1:33.) The righteous, he was told, would hold his name in honor, while the wicked would hold it in reproach. Then Moroni gave Joseph Smith a sign by which he might know that all that he had been told would come to pass. The sign was that when the world learned of the Book of Mormon, they would circulate falsehoods to destroy his reputation and seek to take his life. Yet if he were faithful, he would be preserved to witness the restoration of the priesthood, the ordinance of baptism by water, and the giving of the Holy Ghost by the laying on of hands. "Then will persecution rage more and more," Moroni said, "for the iniquities of men shall be revealed, and those who are not built upon the Rock will seek to overthrow this church; but *it will increase the more opposed.*" (*Messenger and Advocate,* October 1835, 2:199.)

The pattern is well established. Abraham's efforts to be a "greater follower of righteousness" and to more fully "keep the commandments of God" so kindled the wrath of the idolatrous priests of Elkenah that they sought his life and attempted to sacrifice him to their gods. (Abraham 1.) Moses, immediately following his experience on the high mountain, where he had been clothed in the power of God, and had seen the endless expanses of eternity, was confronted by Satan, who "came tempting him, saying: Moses, son of man, worship me." (Moses 1:12.) It was necessary for Moses to witness "the bitterness of hell" before he was to be filled again with the power of God so that he might witness the continuation of the marvelous manifestation. Similarly, it was after Christ had been fasting for forty days and nights that he was challenged by the devil. We learn from the Joseph Smith Translation that he had gone into the wilderness "to be with God" and that he was transported from place to place by the Spirit as Moses had been taken on the high mountain. Satan was but a tagalong who, at the conclusion of each divine lesson, sought to tempt the Master.

The experiences of Christ and the prophets seem to establish the principle or the pattern: "The nearer a person approaches the Lord, a greater power will be manifested by the adversary to prevent the accomplishment of His purposes." (Whitney, *Life of Heber C. Kimball,* p. 132.) There is no spiritual progress without opposition.

Spiritual Sham

Revelation and spiritual experience, like true religion, always have their counterfeits. This is as true within the Church as it is in the world. In greater or lesser degree all of us, as we grow to spiritual maturity, have been tempted with these spiritual shams. Perhaps it would be helpful for us to briefly identify some of their more common forms.

The Spiritual-Bargain Hunters. These are the people who are constantly on the alert for a spiritual sale. They desire salvation without effort or inconvenience. They are often found shopping for counsel, running from Church leader to Church leader seeking answers that justify the course they have already determined to follow. They have mastered the art of selective hearing and selective believing. They continue to shop until they find what they want. These seekers of a bargain-basement theology are offended at the price tag affixed to genuine spiritual experiences and real gospel understanding.

The Saved Mormons. Having had some special spiritual experience or some special relationship with the heavens, these people become resentful when someone disturbs their pleasant spiritual slumber. They have some kinship to those of whom Nephi spoke when he said, "A Bible! A Bible! We have got a Bible, and there cannot be any more Bible." Their motto seems to be "Knowledge! Understanding! We have knowledge and understanding, and there cannot be any more knowledge or understanding." Their attitude is often very condescending toward the rest of the congregation who have not had the same spiritual experiences they claim.

The Spiritual Con Artists. In one of its most insidious forms, the con game is played by someone using Church membership or priesthood position as collateral for a business deal. This sham also includes the many young men and young women who have had dreams or visions in which they have been given specific directions as to whom they are to marry. A frustration to these manipulators of romance is that so many of them receive instructions that they are to marry the same person. One of the identifying characteristics of the spiritual con artists is the seeming ease with which they get answers to their prayers and the freedom with which they communicate with the heavens.

The Crusaders. Always articulate, these self-ordained spokesmen have a mission to straighten the church out on something or other. Often they can trace their authority to some private conversation with one of the Brethren (usually one who is now dead). Not infrequently their pitch will need as part of its introduction an affirmation of their testimony, loyalty to the Church, and positions that they have held. Of such, beware! There is a world of difference between the person who says, "I believe the Church is true and sustain the Prophet, *but* . . ." and the person who says, "I believe the Church is true and sustain the Prophet, *therefore* . . ."

The Goose-Pimple Gang. These are those who ride on an emotional wave. If it brings a tear to your eye or raises the hair on your arms, it must be revelation. They love the sensational and the dramatic but quickly lose interest in the scriptures and the basic principles of the gospel. They cherish "hand-me-down" stories that they hold to tenaciously even when confronted by eyewitnesses who tell them their stories are embellished and inaccurate.

The Destroying Angels. These are those who use gospel principles or leadership positions as a club to beat everyone else into line. These angels of destruction are often found impugning the loyalty and commitment of any whose experience, point of view, or spiritual maturity differs from their own. What they see is all there is to be seen. Like the spiritual mole, instead of building on the rock of revelation, they have burrowed beneath it. These souls have made their Sunday clothes from 100 percent pure woolen zeal. They have yet to find out how much more comfortable it is to wear a garment blended with patience, longsuffering, and love unfeigned.

Spirituality is something to be worked at, not something to be played with. Satan can and does use such expressions as "I feel impressed to say," "It was made known to me," "After much prayer," and "It is the will of the Lord that . . ." Satan, who can speak all languages, also speaks very fluent Mormonese.

Truth can stand on its own. It does not need an office or a position to lean on. It need not be dressed up to appear respectable. It is not enhanced by shows of force, nor is it made more recognizable by emotional displays. Everything that comes from God carries with it its own evidence of its divine origin and needs no artificial coloring to make it more palatable.

All to Receive the Spirit of Revelation and Prophecy

All are entitled to the spirit of revelation and prophecy. This principle was dramatized when Eldad and

Medad, filled with the spirit, prophesied in the camp of Israel. Joshua, fearing that this was out of order, said to Moses, "My lord Moses forbid them." Moses responded, "Enviest thou for my sake? would God that all the Lord's people were prophets, and that the Lord would put his spirit upon them!" (Numbers 11:26-29.) Then as today, Israel was to be "a kingdom of priests," a nation of prophets, one in which "every man might speak in the name of God the Lord, even the Savior of the world." (D&C 1:20.) Teaching the same principle, Paul wrote to the Corinthian saints, saying, "Ye may all prophesy one by one, that all may learn, and all may be comforted." (1 Corinthians 14:31.) Whenever the Spirit of God has been present, the spirit of revelation and prophecy have been present also.

To deny revelation is to deny God. The greatest truths are opposed by the greatest heresies. Few heresies are greater than those which seek to silence God. The Holy Ghost is a revelator. No one can receive the Holy Ghost without receiving revelation. To deny revelation is to deny the Holy Ghost.

What missionary has not had his or her testimony of living prophets rebuffed with the Savior's warning that in the last days there would be false prophets? Yet why the warning? Would we have been warned against false prophets if there were not to be true prophets also? Can there be a counterfeit unless there is a genuine after which it is copied?

A Profile of the Spirit

Describing the characteristics distinctive to the spirit of revelation, James said, "The wisdom that is from above is first pure, then peaceable, gentle, and easy to be intreated, full of mercy and good fruits, without partiality, and without hypocrisy." (James 3:17.) The spirit of revelation does not associate with that which is unclean or impure. It brings with it feelings of peace and assurance; it is gentle and quiet, not showy, loud, or boisterous. The spirit of revelation is never without dignity. It leads, entreats, and encourages, doing so without sham or pretense. Its fruits are good, and it is never a respecter of persons. It is a spirit that invites all to come into the presence of the Lord and "partake of his goodness." It denies none who seek it, be they black or white, bond or free, male or female. It remembers that all are alike unto God. (2 Nephi 26:33.)

To Hyrum Smith the Lord said, "I will impart unto you of my Spirit, which shall enlighten your mind, which shall fill your soul with joy; and then shall ye know, or by this shall you know, all things whatsoever you desire of me, which are pertaining unto things of righteousness, in faith believing in me that you shall receive." (D&C 11:13-14.) Among the distinctive phrases that are a part of our verbal profile of the spirit of revelation are "enlighten your mind" and "shall fill your soul with joy."

Illustrating the first, President Marion G. Romney has said, "I can always tell when I have spoken by the spirit, because I learn something." Peter illustrated the second on the mount of transfiguration, when, after all its glorious manifestations, he turned to the Savior and said, "Lord, it is good for us to be here." (Matthew 17:4.) Such is the feeling that burns within the heart and soul when one has been in the presence of the spirit of revelation.

After his death, Joseph Smith appeared to Brigham Young in a dream and instructed him as follows: "Tell the brethren to be humble and faithful and be sure to keep the Spirit of the Lord, that it will lead them aright. Be careful and not turn away the still, small voice; it will teach them what to do and where to go; it will yield the fruits of the kingdom. Tell the brethren to keep their hearts open to conviction, so that when the Holy Ghost comes to them, their hearts will be ready to receive it. They can tell the Spirit of the Lord from all other spirits—it will whisper peace and joy to their souls; it will take malice, hatred, strive and all evil from their hearts, and their whole desire will be to do good, bring forth righteousness, and build up the kingdom of God." (Manuscript History of Brigham Young, February 23, 1847; as quoted by Marion G. Romney, in *Conference Report*, April 1944, pp. 140-41.)

There are certain feelings that are associated with the Spirit of the Lord and thus attend the spirit of revelation, and others that are alien to it. The Spirit of the Lord is positive, not negative. It is associated with light, not darkness. It leads to remorse for sins but not to discouragement and despair. It brings a broken heart and a contrite spirit but not a sense of worthlessness or meaninglessness. It is associated with faith and courage, not a lack of confidence or a self-demeaning attitude. It is bold but not overbearing; it is strong but not oppressive. Like the power of the priesthood, it is something that can be experienced only in righteousness. It is never associated with hiding sins, gratifying pride, or vain ambition. It seeks no control or dominion in any degree of unrighteousness. Rather it is maintained by gentleness and meekness, by love unfeigned, by kindness, and by pure knowledge, which enlarges the soul without hypocrisy and without guile. (See D&C 121:36-42.) Such is the spirit and such are the blessings after which we seek.

Index

Aaronic Priesthood, 54. *See also*
    Priesthood
Abraham, 43-44, 81, 118-19, 124
Adam, 15, 102, 108, 117
Adamic language, 85
Agency, principle of, 35-38
Alma, 50-51
Aminadi, 62
Ananias, 45-46
Ancient of Days, 108
Ancients, restoring knowledge of,
    109-10
Angels, 14, 42, 38-39, 108-9, 127
Apocrypha, 82-83
Apostles, 13-14, 56-57
Aramaic, 85
Articles of Faith, 120
Atonement, 102-3

Babies, story of, 67
Baptism, 26, 30-31, 53
Bargain hunters, spiritual, 125
Barnabus, letter of, 81-82
Belief, 94, 97-99
Belshazzar, 62-63
Bible: promises continuous revelation,
    3-4; for gaining knowledge, 4-5;
    what, is, 71-72; how, came to be,
    73-77; books of, 77-78, 80-82, 84,
    87; meaning of *testament* in, 78-80;
    Apocrypha in Catholic, 82-84; Dead
    Sea scrolls and, 84-85; language of,
    85-86; original manuscripts of, 86;
    first translation of, 86-87; English
    translation of, 87-90; trusting

translations of, 90-92; Joseph Smith
    translation of, 92-93; as word of
    God, 93; latter-day scriptures on,
    93-94, 107-9; Latter-day Saints'
    belief in, 94; is not the only
    scripture, 95-97; Book of Mormon
    and, 97-98, 102-3; fulfillment of
    prophecies in, 110-11. *See also*
    Scriptures
Book of Abraham, 118-19
Book of Mormon: sealed portion of, 29;
    written for our day, 58-59; lesser
    portion of, 65; purpose of, 93-94; as
    witness, 95-97; as proof, 97-99;
    confounds false doctrines, 99-101;
    Bible and, sustain each other, 102-3;
    as aid to get nearer to God, 103-4.
    See also Scriptures
Book of Moses, 92, 116-18
Brass plates, 74
Buren, Martin van, 16-17
Burroughs, John, 67
Busy, being too, 67-68

Calling through inspiration, 13-14
Catholic Bible, 82-83, 87-89
Channels, priesthood, 45-46
Choices, making, 35-38
Church of Jesus Christ of Latter-day
    Saints, 14, 112-13
Clark, J. Reuben, 68-69
Clement, letter from, 81-82
Coin, sound of, 67
Coming, Second, 61-62, 111-12
Coming forth of Bible, 73-77

Commentary, revealed, 107-9
Compass, spiritual, 50-54
Con artists, spiritual, 126
Confirmation of scriptures, 11-13
Constancy of principles, 69-70
Conversion, 57-58
Cornelius, 21, 38, 46
Council in heaven, 114, 117, 119
Counterfeits, spiritual, 125-27
Covenant, 53-54, 78-79, 118
Cowdery, Oliver, 34, 54, 63-64
Creation, 116-17, 119
Crusaders, 126

Daniel, 62-63, 110
David, 55-56
Dead Sea scrolls, 84-86
Death penalty, 89
Decision-making, 35-38
Destroying angels, 127
Destruction of wicked, 58
Diligence, 40-42
Direction, receiving Lord's, 13-14
Dispensations, 106-7, 113-15
Divination, 49
Doctrine and Covenants: section one,
   7-8, 106; lost records to be restored,
   84; pertinence, 105; voice of
   warning, 106; key to past, 106-7;
   revealed commentary, 107-9;
   restoring knowledge, 109-10;
   prophetic fulfillment, 110-11; guide
   for last days, 111-12; Church
   doctrine and government, 112; duty
   of Saints, 113; we stand independent,
   113. *See also* Scriptures
Doctrines, false, 99-101
Dream of Nebuchadnezzar, 110
Duty of Saints, 113

Edersheim, Alfred, 26, 85
Elijah, 6-7, 111
Elisha, 6-7
Endowment, 53
Engagement, story of, 37
English, Bible translated into,
   87-90
Enlightenment, 129
Enoch, 117-18
Eusebius, 77
Eve, 117
Existence, premortal, 117, 119

Ezekiel, 102
Ezra, 74-75

Face of Lord, seeing, 28
Facsimiles in Book of Abraham, 119
Faith, 39, 52-53, 64-65, 122
Fall of Adam, 102, 117
False doctrines, 99-101
Fasting, 21-22
First Vision, 123-24
Foreshadowing, 110-11. *See also* Types
   and shadows
Foxe, John, 88-89
Freedom from sin, 23-24
Fruit of revelation, 47-48
Fulfillment of prophecy, 110-11
Future, past is prophecy of, 58-59

Genesis, 116
Ginzberg, Louis, 53, 117
Glory, degrees of, 110
God: invitation to ask, 1-3; known only
   by revelation, 4-6; gives revelation to
   groups, 15-16; obedience leads to
   knowing, 24; gives revelation
   according to capacities, 40-42;
   respects stewardship, 46; writing of,
   62-63; Bible is word of, 93; Book of
   Mormon teaches of, 96-97; proof
   that, is unchanging, 98-101; false
   doctrines about, 99-100; getting
   nearer to, 103-4; appearing of, 108;
   revelations of, to Moses, 116-18;
   chose Christ, 117
Goose-pimple gang, 127
Gospel of Peter, 81-82
Gospel taught by Noah, 115
Gospels, 76-77
Government, Church, 14, 112
Greek, 85-87

Hearing of revelation, 66-69
Heart, understanding with, 69
Heaven, 30-32, 108, 114, 117-19
Hebrew, 85
Hebrew Bible. *See* Bible; Old Testament
Heed, giving, 40-42
Helaman, 50-51
Heresy, 88-90, 99-100, 128
Hermas, 82
Holy Ghost: effects of, 12-13; compared
   to broadcasting, 17-18; is revelator,

18, 33, 122; companionship of, 22;
requisites to receiving, 30-32; should
be companion in prayer, 34-35;
reveals mysteries of God, 98-99; will
lead disciples, 129-30. *See also* Spirit
Holy: ground, 24-26; people, 26-29

Independence, 113
Institutional revelation, 10-13
Interpretation of revelations, 60-63
Introduction, Explanatory, to Doctrine
and Covenants, 112
Invitation to ask God, 1-3
Isaiah, prophecies of, 6-7
Israel, 26, 55-56

James, message of, 1-2
James I, 90
Jared, brother of, 29
Jerome Bible, 87-89
Jesse, 55-56
Jesus Christ: gains knowledge, 5-6;
Moses' prophecy of, 8; chose and
instructed Twelve, 13-14;
appearances of, 15, 24-25, 28, 65,
108; has purpose for angels, 38-39;
respects stewardship, 46; guidance
of, 52; word of, is compass, 52-54;
types and shadows of, 55-58;
discourse of, on signs of times, 58,
109; time of coming of, 61-62;
studied Old Testament, 73;
relationship of Gospels to, 76-77;
atonement of, 102-3; announces
Joseph Smith, 106; on mount of
transfiguration, 109; visit of, to spirit
prison, 110; chosen as Redeemer,
117; tempted by Satan, 125
Joel, promise of, 2-3
John the Baptist, 54, 84, 110-11
John the Revelator, 4, 72, 84
Joseph of Egypt, 63, 80
Joseph Smith–History, 119-20
Joseph Smith–Matthew, 119
Joseph Smith translation, 92-93, 116-19
Joshua, 56-57, 128
Josiah, 73-74
Joy, 129

Key to past, 106-7
Kimball, Spencer W., 35, 68
King James Bible, 90

Kirtland, 24-25
Knowledge, 4-6, 42-43, 109-10

Language in scriptures, 6-7, 85-86, 98,
108-9, 127
Last days, 111-12, 119
Latin Vulgate, 87-89
Law, Mosaic, 26-27, 73-75, 79-80
Lee, Harold B., 67-69
Lehi, 50-52, 80
Letters of New Testament, 75-76
Liahona, 49-54
Line upon line, 42-43
Listening, 66-69
Losses to scriptures, 73-74, 80-81,
84-86, 91-92

Manifestations of Spirit. *See* Spirit
Manuscripts of Bible, 86
Marriage, 109
McConkie, Bruce R., 17-18, 20,
24-25, 34
McKay, David O., 67-68
McLellin, William E., 98
Melchizedek Priesthood. *See* Priesthood
Messenger, Joseph Smith as, 110
Miracles, 100-101
Montanus, 78
Mormons, saved, 126
Mosaic, 123
Moses: instructed people to see God,
16; on holy ground, 25; receives
mysteries, 26-28; law of, 26-27,
73-75, 79-80; sends spies, 56-57;
experiences of, on mountain,
114-16, 121; saw Creation, 116-17;
saw ancient patriarchs, 117-18;
Satan confronts, 124-25; rejoices
over prophesying, 127-28. *See also*
Book of Moses
Mysteries, 26-28, 54-58

Nebuchadnezzar, dream of, 110
Negativeness, 130
Nephi, son of Helaman, 23
Nephi, son of Lehi, 65-66, 74, 98-99
Noah, 58, 115, 118
New Testament, 75-80, 86, 92. *See also*
Bible; Scriptures

Oath and covenant, 53-54
Obedience, 24, 69-70

Old Testament, 71-74, 78-81, 84-87. *See also* Bible; Scriptures
Opposition in all things, 123-25

Packer, Boyd K., 67
Past, relationship of revelation to, 58-59, 106-7, 113-15
Patience, 44
Patriarchal blessings, 47, 63
Paul, 45-46, 75-76
Pearl of Great Price: overview, 114-15; Book of Moses, 116-18; Book of Abraham, 118-19; Joseph Smith–Matthew, 119; Joseph Smith–History, 119-20; Articles of Faith, 120
Personal revelation. *See* Revelation
Peter, 38, 46, 81-82
Pharisees, 66-67
Philo, 27
Phoenix, 82
Plan of salvation, 10-11
Pondering revelation, 66
Positiveness of Spirit, 130
Power, spiritual, 23-24
Prayer, 1-2, 34-35, 39-40, 63-64, 67-70
Preexistence, 117, 119
Preparation for Spirit: necessary qualities, 21-22; freedom from sin brings spiritual power, 23-24; holy ground, 24-26; holy people, 26-29; revelation of truth, 29-30; to have heavens opened, 30-32; extent of revelation, 40-41
Priesthood: and revelation, 14; among holy people, 26-28; as requisite to receiving Holy Ghost, 31-32; channels of, 45-46; oath and covenant of, 53-54; restoration of Aaronic, 54; Key-words of, 115
Principles, eternal, 10-11, 20, 35-38, 69-70
Profile of spirit of revelation, 128-30
Progression, 42-43
Promise of revelation, 2-4, 18-19, 43-45
Proof, Book of Mormon as, 97-99
Prophecy, 58-59, 105-6, 108-11, 128-30
Prophets, 4-6, 98, 127-28
Purposes of revelation. *See* Types of revelation

Qualities of spirit of revelation, 129
Qumran, 84-85

Radio, revelation compared to, 17-18
Reason, right, 38-40
Records sustain each other, 102-3
Rejection of revelation, 2-6, 8, 29-30, 96
Restoration, revelations of. *See* Doctrine and Covenants
Resurrection, 110
Revelation: invitation to ask God, 1-3; promises of continuous revelation, 3-4, 8-9; God known only by revelation, 4-6; Joseph Smith's mission foretold, 6-7; no salvation without revelation, 7-8; institutional revelation, 10-13; stewardship revelation, 13-14; shared revelation, 14-16; personal revelation, 16-19, 63-66; applying the principle, 20; qualities to receive revelation, 21-22; freedom from sin brings spiritual power, 23-24; holy ground, 24-26; holy people, 26-29; revelation of truth, 29-30; to have heavens opened, 30-32; scriptural study, 33-34, 63-64; get the Spirit, 34-35; agency principle, 35-38; right reason, 38-40; heed and diligence, 40-42; line upon line, 42-43; right time, 43-45; priesthood channels, 45-46; sacred silence, 46-47; revelation begets revelation, 47-48; devices for revelation, 49-50; personal Liahona, 50-51; types and shadows, 51-52; word of Christ, 52-54; unfolding mysteries, 54-58; past is prophecy of future, 58-59; Spirit is same forever, 59; understanding revelation, 60-63, 69; all may hear, 66-69; principles are constant, 69-70; promise of manifestations of Spirit, 121-23; opposition in all things, 123-25; spiritual sham, 125-27. *See also* Bible; Book of Mormon; Doctrine and Covenants; Holy Ghost; Pearl of Great Price; Scriptures; Spirit
Revelation, spirit of, 34, 69, 127-30
Righteousness, 21, 52-53
Romney, Marion G., 129

Sadducees, 66-67
Saint Peter's Basilica, 123
Saints, Latter-day, 14-16, 94, 112-13
Salvation and revelation: invitation to

ask God, 1-3; Bible promises
continuous revelation, 3-4; God
known only by revelation, 4-6;
Joseph Smith's mission foretold, 6-7;
no salvation without revelation, 7-8;
scriptures promise personal
revelation, 8-9; plan of salvation,
10-11; salvation not by spiritual
experiences, 39-40; progression in
knowledge of salvation, 42-43
Samuel, 55-56
Sanctification, 26-29, 32
Sarah, 43-44
Satan, 116-17, 123-25, 127
Saved Mormons, 126
Scott, Richard, 36-37
Scriptures: acceptance of, 4-5; promise
personal revelation, 8-9; as
institutional revelation, 10-13; using,
20; study of, 33-34, 63-65, 122-23;
as compass, 54; types and shadows
in, 54-58; value of, 59; help to
understand revelation, 70; loss of,
73-74, 80-81; read aloud to Judah,
74-75; decision on closing canon of,
78; missing, to be restored, 84;
errors in, 91-92; what latter-day, say
about Bible, 93-94; power of,
121-22; and voice of Lord, 122; as
mosaic, 123. *See also* Bible; Book of
Mormon; Doctrine and Covenants;
Joseph Smith translation; Pearl of
Great Price
Scrolls for Old Testament, 72
Secrets of heaven, 26-28
Seeking of revelation. *See* Revelation
Seer stones, 49, 59
Septuagint Bible, 83, 86-87
Sham, spiritual, 125-27
Shared revelation, 14-16
Shepherd of Hermas, 81-82
Sign seekers, 39-40
Signs of the times, 58, 109, 111-12
Silence, sacred, 46-47
Sin, freedom from, 23-24
Smith, Hyrum, 69, 122-23
Smith, Joseph: on salvation, 1; and
James's message, 1-2; on revelation,
3, 19, 49, 60-61, 64, 105; mission of,
foretold, 6-7; on gift of Holy Ghost,
10; on Holy Ghost, 12, 33; on
differences of Mormonism, 16-17;
scripture study led, to revelation, 34;

on following and enquiring of God,
40; on sacred silence, 47; in
restoration of Aaronic Priesthood,
54; as type for conversion, 57-58;
prays to know time of Christ's
coming, 61-62; asks his brother for
decision, 69; on truth, 69; restored
ancient texts, 81; inquired about
Apocrypha, 83; on Bible translation,
90-91; on Mormon belief in Bible,
94; Book of Mormon as proof that,
is prophet, 98; challenges William E.
McLellin, 98; on Book of Mormon,
104-5; voice of warning introducing,
106; on present dispensation, 107;
on gazing into heaven, 108; as
messenger, 110; on spirits, 111; as
leader of Church, 112; and Pearl of
Great Price, 115; history of, 119-20;
on faith, 122; on efforts of Satan,
123-24; name of, 124; in dream,
129-30. *See also* Joseph Smith
translation
Smith, Joseph F., 34
Smith, Joseph Fielding, 28-29
Snow, Lorenzo, 19
Spirit: attends holy places, 25-26; get
the, 34-35; is forever same, 59; gives
interpretation, 63; promise of
manifestations of, 121-23; opposition
to, in all things, 123-25; spiritual
shams concerning, 125-27; all to
receive, and prophecy, 127-28;
profile of, 128-30. *See also* Holy
Ghost
Spirit of revelation. *See* Revelation,
spirit of
Spirits, 110-11
Spiritual: power, 23-24; experiences,
46-47; compass, 52-54; bargain
hunters, 125; con artists, 126
Spirituality, 127
Stake president, man called as, 36-37
Standard works, 10-13, 20
Stewardship revelation, 13-14, 45-46
Sticks of Joseph and Judah, 102-3
Study, scriptural, 33-34, 63-65, 122-23
Synagogue worship, 73

Taylor, John, 105
Television, revelation compared to,
17-18
Temples, 24-25, 28-29

Testament, meaning of, 78-80
Time, right, 43-45
Times, signs of. *See* Signs of the times
Transfiguration, mount of, 109
Translation: Oliver Cowdery attempts,
    63-64; first, of Bible, 86-87; English,
    of Bible, 87-90; trusting, of Bible,
    90-92; Joseph Smith, of Bible,
    92-93; of Book of Abraham, 118
Truth, 11-13, 29-30, 97-98, 127
Tyndale, William, 87, 89-90
Types and shadows, 51-52, 54-55
Types of revelation: institutional
    revelation, 10-13; stewardship
    revelation, 13-14; shared revelation,
    14-16; personal revelation, 16-19;
    applying the principle, 20

Unchangeableness of God, 98-101
Understanding of revelation, 60-61;
    revelation necessary to, 61-63;
    demands study, 63-64; requires
    faith, 64-65; growing into, 65-66;
    willingness in, 66-69; with the heart,
    69; principles in, are constant, 69-70
Union of Bible and Book of Mormon,
    102-3

Urim and Thummim: devices for
    revelation, 49-50; personal Liahona,
    50-51; types and shadows, 51-52;
    word of Christ as compass, 52-54;
    unfolding mysteries, 54-58; past is
    prophecy of future, 58-59; Spirit is
    same forever, 59; Doctrine and
    Covenants, 107; Pearl of Great
    Price, 114-15

Visions, 2-3, 60-61. *See also* Revelation
Voice of Lord, 106, 122
Vulgate, 87-89

Warning, voice of, 106
Wellington, Mount, 17
Wells, John, 67-68
Witness, necessity for personal, 8-9
Witness, second. *See* Book of Mormon
Woodruff, Wilford, 38-39
Word of Christ, 52-54, 93, 95-97
Works, righteous, 21-22, 30-31
Worship, scriptures in, 73
Writing on wall, 62
Wycliffe, John, 88-89

Young, Brigham, 14, 19, 41-42, 93-94,
    129-30